Where to find Customers
when you run out of
Family and Friends

the
Lemon Aid
Lead Alphabet

Christie Northrup
The Lemon Aid Lady

Cover Design by Steve James

PUBLISHED BY CANet Publishing

Printed in the United States of America

ISBN: 1-930182-01-5

Dedicated to
Bob

...my editor, best friend, teammate, and husband whose continual encouragement and support teaches me how to twist sour situations into sweet successes.

Lemon Aid Lead Alphabet
Laws for
Locating Leads

1. **LLL:** **Look**...for people who need and/or want you
   and/or your product.

   Listen...to what they say.

   Learn...about who they are and what their
   needs, wants, desires, and interests are.

2. **MM:** Develop a
   Matchmaker
   Mentality.

3. **HO HO:** Hang Out
   where your leads
   Hang Out.

4. **BB:** Be Bold – talk to people, ask questions, invite
   them to do business with you.

LEADS ARE THE SEEDS OF YOUR BUSINESS...

You are the owner of your own business. You sell directly to a consumer. You might sell insurance, satellite dishes, information, make up, vitamins, candles, software, or a myriad of other products and services. But, selling directly to consumers is the most beneficial way of marketing because you are able to develop one-on-one relationships with lifetime clients, and they come to know you as "their" professional. You give exceptional customer service to your clients; they almost become family to you. And because direct selling is a relationship business, customer retention is high-- sometimes even through generations.

Of course, the benefit to you is unlimited earning potential and the luxury of working when you want, where you want, and at the level of activity and income you want.

But, what if you don't already have those relationships? What if you're new to the business? What if you've run out of family and friends as prospects--or didn't have any to begin with? Where do you go? How to you build a life-long business?

You are holding the seed to your future in your hands right now. The Lemon Aid Lead Alphabet will give you simple-to-use suggestions on who to contact, how to contact, what to say, and how to follow through. You will find hundreds of seeds which will turn to leads which will turn to a harvest of business for you. And, as you plant and nourish these seeds into leads and into business, you will find your own seeds. The most important way to continue to build a thriving business is to share your new ideas and successful experiences with others.

As you plant these seeds, remember that planting is the first step-- not the only one and not the last one. Just like planting a flower or vegetable seed, work, effort, and time are key elements. Always be aware of those that say you'll be rich overnight. Real harvests require constant nourishing. In the beginning, you will do a lot of activities that you might not get paid for. However, as your business grows, you'll get paid for a lot of activities that you didn't do--business will flow to you. Like the lemon tree, you'll be able to harvest your fruits while new business--blossoms--are beginning. You'll never have a dormant season!

As a twenty-year veteran in direct selling, I've had opportunities to enter new areas and build large customer bases as well as recruit and train members of a sales team. I have lived both in small towns and large metropolitan areas. And, one thing I've learned is if you always begin with the right attitude and enthusiasm, people everywhere are very receptive to having you as "their" _____lady or man. You'll become famous---and wealthy---in both tangible and intangible rewards.

The road will sometimes be rocky. At times you'll want to give up. That is why I developed the Lemon Aid Seminars. Direct selling and owning your own business can be the best of times and the worst of times--sometimes on the same day! The key is to learn from your experiences and move on. You will meet many people who will tell you that you won't make it. Do not let anyone destroy your dreams, just pick yourself up by turning to some of the seeds in this book.

To your *Sweet* Successes and Juicy Profits,

Christie Northrup
The Lemon Aid Lady

HOW TO USE THIS BOOK:

You can read this book from cover to cover to glean an overview of many ways to find leads. Or, you can just pick it up and read the first page that falls open. Maybe for a *TWIST,* you can spell something out, such as your name, and then take one or more suggestions from each of the letters in this word or name that you've chosen.

For example, if you think of the word S U C C E S S, go to the S section. Choose one or more ideas from this section. Then go to the U, C, and E sections. As you become familiar with this Lead Alphabet, you will find some seeds yield more and better leads for you. Even though I have personally tried these ideas at one time or another in my career, I recommend you don't go in too many directions at one time. Work on one suggestion for at least a week or more, and when you have that one working, add the next one.

You should never put all your fruit in one basket. Eventually you will want to incorporate many different ways of finding leads into your business. For example, if you tried to get all your leads from the telephone book, you'll become bored, and maybe even discouraged. Add some other seeds for variety. Observe the Lemon Aid Laws for Locating Leads found in the front of this book. Soon, the leads will be flowing, and you'll be developing new ways to build your business.

Throughout the book, you'll notice space to write down your own ideas and experiences for finding leads. Keep a record of all these, and soon your Lead Alphabet will become your personal business handbook.

When you discover new seeds that are bringing you leads, share them. I'll be publishing subsequent Lead Alphabets and would love to incorporate your ideas and successes. Just e-mail them to lemonaidlady@yahoo.com or send to CANet Consulting, P.O. Box 1720, Lake Dallas, Texas 75065-1720. Or call my office at 1-940-498-0995.

Finally, just planting a seed will not produce a harvest. *Follow through* is the next continual step to your success. Nourish and love those leads—and you'll have a bountiful basket of business. More information on this is found in the second Lemon Aid book, *The Lemon Aid Deed Alphabet: The Deeds you Need to Convert Leads to Long-Term Customers and Residual Profits.*

What do **TWIST** and **NAPEF** mean?

In the Lemon Aid Seminars, I teach the key to turn sour situations in Sweet Successes and Juicy Profits is in the *TWIST*--**The Way I See Things.** By changing your perspective just a bit, you'll shed a whole new light on a situation and come up with ideas you never would have thought of. By doing the *TWIST,* you'll turn the same old stuff into Sweet, ongoing Successes. Many examples of this are given throughout the book.

Have you heard of the newest fruit--**NAPEF?** This is actually a hybrid of five fruits: Name, Address, Phone number, E-mail, Fax. I've found that people get all excited about talking to a prospect and tell them "call me if you're interested." This is the biggest mistake I've seen in selling. Always, always, always, get at least the name and phone number of all prospects. This can be done in a very professional, non-threatening way. Something I've used before is, "I'll be happy to provide you with more information if you share your name and phone number." Rarely has anyone declined my offer; I made it too appealing; the prospect could tell I really cared about *them,* not selling something. You can request the address, e-mail and fax numbers at your next contact.

All direct selling business have their own language. In this book, I use the term *consultant* to refer to the person who represents the company to the public. Even if you hold a management position in your company, you probably are a consultant as well.

Many companies use some sort of a demonstration to present their product/service/business plan. Thus, *demonstration* in this book can mean party, show, class, workshop, business presentation, etc.

Recruits and *Recruiting* will be used in this book to mean bringing, or sponsoring, someone into your company or organization.

A

Advertising

In this business, the best kind of advertising is **word-of-mouth**. That's why direct selling is so effective. Inexpensive, target advertising can work in some cases; however, the return ratio is not high, so don't get discouraged. Just keep working. If you do want to pay for advertising, make it simple to read, understand, and respond to. Use catchy headlines that call for immediate action.

When you read the heading of this section, did you think you'd be writing, placing, and paying for ads? That's what comes to the minds of most people. We're going to do a *TWIST* on this approach.

First, **take advantage of the advertising of others.** Be aware of potential customers who need your product because of what *they* sell. For example, if you sell items for use in the kitchen, contact people who are advertising catering services, cooking schools, or restaurants. You'll find ads for these businesses in the newspapers, direct mail pieces, and telephone books, just to mention a few. Another potential customer base would be someone who sells makeup or crafts. They might need something to carry their smaller products in. Could you fill their need? If so, you might even be able to do some cross promoting with them.

Classified Advertising. Many people list their services here. Someone seeking children for their day care would be a prime prospect if you sell anything related to children such as books, toys, software, and so on. If the advertiser listed her name, personalize the phone call by using it.

"Hi, Jane, this is _____(your name) from _____(your company). I saw an ad in the paper about your day care service (this will get her attention!). Since you work with children, I have

products that will help you _____(list the benefits for her)."
From here, you would want to arrange to take a catalog and/or sample of your product to her. This way you begin to develop a business relationship.

People who already have home-based businesses many times are open to other and/or new business opportunities. After all, they may feel like they are running low on customers or they wouldn't be advertising in the paper. Recruit them and invite them to read this book!

Also see: bulletin boards, cross promoting, flyers, headlines, jewel mail

Airplanes

On an airplane, you have a captive audience. Most people **meet their seatmates** and usually inquire about each other's livelihoods. Be prepared with literature and business cards and get their NAPEF. Perhaps the person is flying from your city and can give you referrals for people he or she knows in your town as well as his/her own.

I have scheduled successful demonstrations through people I've met on airplanes. One flight out of Detroit to my town of Midland, Michigan was only 30 minutes long. However, I had enough time to visit with a man who told me to call his wife about my product. He was so intrigued with what I told him about my business opportunity that he wanted his wife to join my team. Although she did not choose that option, she had a great demonstration with me, and I was able to meet some new customers.

Always **leave some of your literature** in the seat pockets where the magazines are kept. Or, **put the literature inside the on-board publications.** Leave a note informing the readers that you can do business with them no matter where they live.

Apartments

Check with owners or renters of apartment complexes to see if you can get some exposure with the tenants. Many complexes have clubhouses where **flyers can be posted.** Also, ask if they have **tenant newsletters** that you can advertise in. Complexes that are locally owned might trade advertising for your product.
Ask if you can use the **clubhouse to set up a product display.**

Get to know the managers. **Ask for an ongoing list of people moving in and out.** For those moving in, you can offer an apartment-warming demonstration. The people moving out might be moving to their first home, and may really need your product (when you move to a new home don't you want everything new?). Both of these groups would be great recruit prospects.

Also see: advertising, bartering, events, mailing lists

Attention Getters

This is any way of **getting people to ask you** about your product or service. See: badges, bulletin boards, flyers, grocery stores, headlines, logo wear, magnets

Auto Repair Shops

Have you been to one of these lately? Usually the magazines in the waiting room are targeted only to men. What about something for women as well (especially those who love to shop from catalogs like yours!) Of course, you will want men to shop too. Ask the owner of the shop for permission to set up a display easel to put your catalogs in, then go a step further: put a box with a tear pad for prospects to write their name, address, phone number, and areas of interest. These can be printed inexpensively at a local printer. Offer a monthly drawing for a product gift certificate. If the owner needs an incentive, offer some of your products as a thank you for allowing you to use this space. If you don't want to put up a display easel, at least leave a trail of catalogs or other literature.

Also see: displays, literature, waiting room

B

Badges

Badges with catchy sayings will cause people to be *curious* about your business and *ask you* what the badge means. A question on the badge is even more effective than just a statement because people will *come to you* with an answer or comment. You're going to go to the store, volunteering at school, taking a walk with your family, and doing other everyday activities anyway, so you might as well give your business some fun, easy, and profitable exposure at the same time. You never know who has been looking for you and your product! The Booster at 1.800.5JENNYB has a great selection at inexpensive prices.

Badge with your company name on it. If your company provides you with a name tag/badge, wear it! This is a great attention getter! When you're walking down the aisles of a store, aren't you attracted to people with name tags? Why? Because those people stand out from the rest. You have a great product/service/business, you deserve to stand apart from the crowd as well. As you approach this person with the name tag, you probably think they work at that store. As you get closer, you notice the name tag is not what the employees in the store are wearing. So, you look even closer, right? This is human nature. Always wear this when you're out and about and look dressed to do business. A word of caution: don't wear your company badge if you're not dressed for business because first impressions are lasting; you'll give the wrong impression of your normally-professional image.

Combining your company badge with a creative badge also works well. Some of my most fun business experiences happened when I'd be stopping at the store on my way home, not even thinking about my business, and someone would stop and ask me how they could do business with me! *Also see: name tags*

Bake Sales

Mothers hate bake sales! First they have to bake the products, and then they go buy them back--just to help fund a worthwhile cause for their children! Approach the people running the bake sale about doing a fund raiser with you and your product! All parents will appreciate you and the break from baking!

Also see: fund raisers

Banks

You'll be visiting the bank often when you use the ideas in this book. You'll be making bigger and more frequent deposits. Get to know all the people at all the branches of your bank. Every time you make a deposit of your profits, let the teller know what the check is for. Let him/her know what you did to earn the check, how much fun you had, and how much time it took. "I earned this $300 check in two hour's time by teaching two other people how to do my job. Now I have two new friends and the opportunity to earn bigger profits!" Believe me, she/he will be very curious! In fact, this is one of the best ways to get leads for recruiting! After all, they are seeing the checks and the money you are making-- they'll want to know how they can share in the wealth.

Drive Through. When you're in a hurry and must drive through to do your banking, be sure to give the teller a gift of your sales literature. This is a TWIST on what most people do; they ask the tellers for suckers for the kids. The tellers will remember you because you *gave* them something very valuable.

Customers' Banks. If you want to expand your banking contacts, take a check written from one of your customers and go directly to their bank to cash it. The employees there will not know you, so you will have to show identification. This is another perfect time to tell them about you and your business. Because you might not go to that bank again, be sure to get the NAPEF of the persons you talk to. Offer them the free service of bringing a display into their lunch room so they can shop on site.

Also see: drive through

Barter

This is **trading your product/service** for the product/service of another. This not only saves on cash flow, but also adds more customers to your base. When you are in need of a product/service, go to a person in that business and suggest bartering. This way both of you have a new customer and can also cross-promote each other's business through referrals. This works well for any two people who are willing to trade. Just be sure you both keep good records and receipts. Check with your tax advisor; bartering can be subject to income tax.

You can barter for services and products you use in your business (advertising, printing, office supplies, etc.) as well as items needed in your personal life. For years, I did not pay cash for any hair services or manicures for me or my family. Everything was through bartering! At one point, my hairdresser was remodeling her home. She traded for everything from counter tops to windows to carpets! My good friend and business assistant, Kim Barker, not only worked for me, but she also ran a wonderful preschool in her home. Kim had a copier for all the preschool papers. I also needed copying done for my team, hostesses, and customers. So, we traded copying for my product. She, in turn, traded tuition for her preschool for photography, draperies, craft items, and more! I've also traded for music lessons and products from other direct sales representatives. Bartering broadens your business base!

Bartering for child care. Once in a while I had to have someone care for my children while I had a business appointment. I didn't need the full-time services of a daycare center, so I asked a neighbor or a customer who enjoyed children and loved my product. In place of paying them an hourly fee in cash, I paid the fee with my product. Through the years, the ladies that cared for my children with this arrangement loved it!!

Remember to **trade retail price for retail price.** This way you both end up getting the other's service at your wholesale cost; you'll never pay retail again!

Also see: cross promoting

Bath Room Stalls

Anywhere you can have a captive audience, go for it!! Hang a business card flyer inside the bathroom stall doors. The cleaning people might take the flyer off the door, but you'll have an audience for a little while. Always keep a couple of flyers and a roll of tape in your briefcase or purse so you have the tools handy. This technique can easily be done in the course of your daily routine.

Also see: business card flyer

Beauty Salons/Barber Shops

This is another place where people normally have to wait, either for an appointment or while sitting under the dryer. Have some sales and recruiting information, and a company magazine available for them to look at.

Also see: bartering, displays, resource centers, waiting areas

Bumper Stickers

I've seen bumper stickers on the cars of consultants from many direct sales companies. One suggestion is to put your phone number on the bumper sticker.

While driving down the freeway one day, I noticed a bumper sticker of a company that I wanted to do business with. I was close enough to read the bumper sticker, but I had no way of contacting the person short of calling the Department of Motor Vehicles and seeing if I could track him down!

If a potential customer has no way of contacting you, all your efforts are futile. Make sure customers can easily get in touch with you.

Also see: cars

Business Associates

This group is the **people you work with.** When you start a direct sales business, you might already have another job. Your new business is a vehicle for you to try a new career and make an additional stream of income. Let those with whom you work know that you can now service the needs they have related to your product. And, as they see your success, they will be prime recruiting candidates.

Also, try to remember **any other place you or your spouse have worked,** and contact those people as well.

Business Cards

Business cards provide a professional image. They are also very inexpensive. **Make a goal to give out a certain number of your business cards each day.** Leave a trail of business cards everywhere you go!

Whenever you are asked to give someone your name, address, etc. when doing a business transaction (dry cleaners, doctors, etc.), give **them a business card rather than dictating your information.** Many stores are asking for your zip codes so they can track where their customers live. Give them your card; let it create some curiosity!

Hand your business card out with all your transactions. When you hand a cashier your payment, give her a business card with it. When you leave a restaurant, leave your card along with a tip. Whenever you meet someone, give them a card!

Enclose a business card with ALL your correspondence; even when mailing bills. Real people open mail; you never know who has been waiting for you to appear! If you're sending personal letters, send your business card along to remind your friends and family about your business.

Be sure your **card looks professional** with your company's logo your name, address, phone, fax, and e-mail address.

Always ask for a business card in return for yours if the atmosphere is conducive to that (a grocery clerk probably doesn't have a business card handy to exchange but an administrative assistant would).

Free lunch drawings - Many restaurants are offering these. You put your business card in the fish bowl, and you might win a free lunch. Do a TWIST on this one. Put a note on the front of your card offering them something free *if they call you and ask about your product/service!* Write the note with a different color of pen so the writing will stand out. Using attention-getting stickers is even a better idea because they can be *felt* not just seen.

Another TWIST: **Ask the restaurant owner what is done with the cards after the drawing. Ask him/her to give you the cards so you can do a "bonus" drawing--your product.** You will have a lot of new names and will know more about the prospect from the information you see on the business card.

If a restaurant doesn't already sponsor a drawing, see if you can sponsor one. Agree to buy a gift certificate for the price of lunch. You can begin by doing a monthly drawing to keep your costs down, but do gather the cards at least once a week. This is an inexpensive way to collect a lot of names. Remember, these people are not a "target" audience--yet. You can go through the cards, and depending on your product, and with the information you know about them from the card, you can sift through and contact them.

Remember the e-mail and fax numbers - a great way to send information in advance of your calling them.

You can target businesses other than restaurants depending on your product. For example, if you sell health food items, talk to a health club. If you sell books, talk to a library. If your target audience is parents, go to where parents hang out--pre-schools, doctor's offices, etc.

Drawings at your Demonstrations/Presentations:
At the end of your demonstration of products or presentation of your business plan, ask everyone to take out their business cards. On the back, have them write a number between one and ten (one being the lowest, ten the highest) indicating their interest in joining

your organization and/or scheduling a demonstration with you.

Why use this card in place of a traditional drawing slip? People like to feel important. By giving you one of their professional cards, they are letting you know their position at the company. This helps them to feel important. The benefit to you is now you know what company they work for, what their position is, and you have their business NAPEF. This information helps you get to know them better.

Recruiting Tip. Do a survey and see if anyone has "president," "owner," or "CEO" listed on their card. If everyone chuckles when you ask this, the answer is most likely no. Let them know that when they join your organization, they ARE the president, owner, and CEO of their own business. And, if applicable, they can keep their titles of mother or father at the same time!

What if they do not have a business card? Give them one of yours--either one with your information on it or a generic one with just your company name. Have them fill out the information themselves and give it back to you. This works well for recruiting. For example, if they don't have a business card, let them know they can have some printed up when they join your organization. Tell them their title in your organization is President of their own business. Do a commercial for owning their own business this way.

Magnetize your business card if you want people to keep your card. The best way is to purchase sheets of magnets. These are usually less expensive at a craft store rather than an office supply store. Using rubber cement, mount the card on the magnet sheet, cut, and you have a business card they'll keep.

Put both sides to work for you. On the reverse side of the card, offer something FREE if the person calls you. Leave a place to hand write an expiration date. If you sell books, you could offer a free story time; software, a free demonstration; toys, a free 30 min play time; kitchenware, a personalized kitchen consultation; makeup, a make over. You might already offer these services on an ongoing basis; however, when you present this in a "special offer" manner, this service becomes even more valuable.

Bookmarks. I read a lot, and business cards make great

bookmarks. When I put them in books I've checked out of the library, my card becomes another way of meeting people. The next person who checks out the book has a free bookmark along with my business card! Hand write a note that encourages them to call you, such as "Redeem this card for 10% off your first purchase."

The last word about business cards: **Before handing them out, hand write the words "thank you" on the back.** You're thanking people in advance for doing business with you; people love that personal touch!!

Also see: library, networking, restaurants

Business Card Flyer

You've seen flyers hanging in the local stores. Someone produces an ad, then on the very bottom of the page, types or writes a phone number that you can tear off. What is wrong with this? I always lose the itty bitty piece of paper, or I save the paper but don't know what it is for! Here's a much better way, that is also eye-catching. Do your flyer, but across the bottom, staple your business cards in a row (one staple per card to make taking the card off easy). People will be drawn to your ad, and when they have your business card, most likely they will call you!

Also see : advertising, bulletin boards, headlines

Bulletin Boards

Most direct selling professionals think of putting up flyers and ads on bulletin boards. Yes, that is one way to attract leads. But, let's do the TWIST on this one: **Call people who are advertising their business or services. How can you help them?** Could you do some cross-promoting with their business? Could your product help them sell their product? Are they happy with their current business, or would they like to hear what you have to offer in addition, or instead of, what they are currently involved in. This is a TWIST on looking for new opportunities! Get in the habit of looking for bulletin boards at stores, libraries, community centers, and so forth.

Bills

Put a flyer, business card, or catalog in the envelopes when paying your bills. These companies gave you sales information when they sent the bill to you, so return the favor.

Bingo

In many parts of the country, people flock to Bingos and spend a lot of money playing the game. Do a TWIST on this and have them come to see your products and play bingo--at no cost to them. You can purchase Bingo supplies at party outlet stores. For the prizes, use excess inventory. To make this more fun, combine the efforts of other consultants in your company. The more the merrier. This is a great opportunity to talk about your company's selling opportunity. People get caught up in the fun and excitement and want to be a part of it all!

MY OWN LEAD-GENERATING IDEAS:

C

Campgrounds

When you do finally get away from it all, take some of it with you. That means always using your product to be a living advertisement. If you enjoy the outdoors, going camping is a great release. This is also opportunity for informal business contacts-- ones that can open many doors.

If you camp at a campground, you know you're not really getting away from it all. You have neighbors that are actually closer than the ones next door at home. But, because the atmosphere is so relaxed, people don't seem to mind. In fact, because the stress level is so low, meeting others and visiting is really enjoyable. Invariably the conversation will turn to asking where you are from and what you do for a living. If you have a product/service that you are using while on this get-away trip, all the better. If not, get the name and phone number of your new friend(s) and be sure to contact them when you get back to the real world. A relaxed atmosphere can really be a blessing and advertisement for your business.

Car

If you are like most people, you are in your car at least once a day; usually more. Here are some ideas that can be working for you even while you're running around.

Hang a sign on your window. This can be a very simple sign you make on your computer (don't hand write it!). Make your product name, your name, and phone number big enough so people can read it when you're driving down the street. You can also order magnetic signs that stick to the side of your car door, check the phone book for possible vendors. People who have been looking for a representative from your company will be thrilled to see your signs. You can gather new leads just from driving around town or while being parked.

Keep some of your product in the rear window of your car
so when your car is parked, people can see a display (this is only if your product won't get damaged from the sun and heat). Be sure that you have your name and number where people can see it so they can contact you.

If putting your product in the back window isn't practical, leave your **catalog and other literature in the back window** so people can see what you sell. Be sure your name and number are visible.

Hang a **mini-poster** in the back or side windows (be sure your view is not obstructed) that reads "To buy or sell_____(your product), call _____(your name and number)"

Do you have a **windshield shade** that is blank on one side? Write a large advertisement for your product. For a real TWIST, put your product **catalogs or literature under your windshield wiper** blades so interested persons can take something of yours with them.

A consultant I know joined her company because she noticed a **license plate holder** with the logo and name of a company she was interested in. She wrote a note for the car's owner and asked for a return phone call.

Bumper stickers with your company's logo/saying. One personal experience about a bumper sticker. My husband and I were stopped at a red light. The car in front of us had a bumper sticker that said "If you want to make money every time you pick up the phone, call me." Well, the offer sounded unique, and I wanted some more information. But, guess what? No where on the bumper sticker did I see a phone number! How was I going to call him? My husband sped up faster and said that if we gently rear ended his car, then we could get his name and phone number! Don't make it hard for your interested prospects to contact you. If your company has any kind of bumper sticker, check to be sure you have a place to write in your phone number.

Whichever car methods you choose to use, be sure people can clearly see your phone number and company name. This way,

14

even when you're driving down the freeway, a potential customer/recruit will know how to get in touch with you. A word of caution, however. Be sure that you display your very best driving manners whenever you use these ideas.

One day I was driving through a small town. The speed limit was 25 miles through the whole city. A truck from a lawn sprinkling system company tailgated me the entire distance of the city and made gestures for me to move over! I was simply obeying the law. Now, do you think I'd ever call that company to install my sprinklers? Wouldn't it have been funny if it had been MY house that he was driving to. He wouldn't have had a job in that town after all.

If your company provides you with a company car, or if you purchased your car with your business profits, let the people know that. You can get some really good recruit referrals that way.

Car Washes

When you see an organization doing a car wash as a fund raising project, pull in and have the group wash your car. Then, ask them how much money they made so far. Normally, the amount is minimal. Find out who the supervisor or advisor to the group is, and let them know about your fund raiser and how they can earn money with your product/service.

Also see: Fund Raisers

Chiropractors

See: waiting rooms

Christmas Card List

You think you've talked to everyone, and that all your leads have been exhausted. Wait... here's a rather warm prospect list that you can do a TWIST with. You normally send Christmas Cards to everyone on your Christmas Card list. Think up your own holiday and make up a card to send to all these people. Type up a letter, just like you might for Christmas. Tell them about the happenings of your family and what's going on in your life. And, of course, tell them about your business. Send along your business card and any literature you have that would make sense to mail. You never know just which one of these acquaintances have been trying to find a consultant from your company. This would also be a good time to ask them for a referral. Suggest that they e-mail you with their orders/referrals/questions. And, let them know you're interested in what they are involved in. With so many people starting in the direct selling business, you might find a good support system as well as customers/recruits from this group of people.

Also see: Distance Customers

Cleaning Professionals

You'll usually find these people listed in the classified section of your paper under Services. This is another TWIST on using someone else's advertising money to promote your business. Why would you contact someone who cleans homes and offices professionally?

1. You might have a product that they need for their business.

2. They could be potential associates for cross promoting
3. They usually work at odd hours--late in the evening--and could possibly have time for another business and might desire the additional stream of income that will help them, and you, with reasons one and two.

Clubs

People join clubs for friendship and service. Most clubs meet on a monthly basis. The person planning the meetings sometimes has a difficult time coming up with interesting agendas. Here's where you come into the picture. **You volunteer to be the guest speaker at their next meeting.** Here are the steps:

1. First, you need to **find the clubs that want you.** Write down

on a piece of paper this question: Who Cares? Then, check out your local newspaper. Most papers have a weekly section listing clubs and their meeting times, places, topics and contact person. Sometimes this section is listed as "community calendar".

2. **Read each club's notes carefully.** The group's name might not tell you the entire story. Read about the kinds of topics they are addressing. What could you offer to enhance this topic that is related to your business?

3. **Call the contact person.** Let them know which company you represent. Tell the person that you're interested in putting on a free seminar dealing with how to_____. Use your creativity in adapting your topic and expertise to their needs.

4. At the seminar, **do not try to sell anything.** This is a chance to create some goodwill.

5. **Use this time to get leads.** Do a drawing so that you have everyone's name, address, phone. Ask what they liked best about your presentation, what they would change (this gives great feedback for your next presentation), and if they would like to know more about this subject. Remember to ask for referrals, too!

6. The drawing gift will be your product/service. You'll be able to **see who is really interested**, especially those who don't win the drawing and are really disappointed.

7. People will come up after and tell you how appreciative they are for the information. At that time, t**he climate is good for giving out your business card.** Those who have high interest will tell you so. Or, you'll find out through questions. If they have a specific request, write that down on their drawing slip; let them see you write it so they know they will receive preferential treatment from you.

8. Of course, the **follow through is critical** on this. Just like any other lead-generating idea, you can get snowed under with leads from here, or, possibly, have none. The key is to **find out what is working and do more of it.**

Also see: newspapers, organizations

Commonalities

When you meet new people, ask them questions about **them.** As they share their information with you, mentally figure out what you might have in common with them. This could be your home town, college you attended, organizations you both belong to, on and on. The key is to **listen to them**. When you find some common ground, acknowledge this to your new friend. All of a sudden, a bond is created! And, the person is now even more open to listening to you!

I have been blessed with three sons, no daughters, (I call my husband Fred McMurray from the TV show, My Three Sons). Whenever I meet someone who has ALL boys, no girls, I create a bond with this person. This is usually the first time I've met them. In fact, I made up a club, The MOB club which stands for Mothers of Boys. When I meet a mother of all boys, I tell them that they are in my club! Many, many times, people would ask, "When does your club meet?" The club exists only in my mind, but because I acknowledge this commonality to another person, and get to know them a little bit better, I begin a relationship that eventually leads to friendships as well as business transactions, in many, many cases.

Consulting

Offer a free consultation about your service/product. This is a low-key way to make an impressive one-on-one presentation. Many people say "no" to something they really want/need because they think that just having you explain the system to them will cost money.

Call your presentation a "no-fee consultation". This is less threatening than saying "let's set up an appointment so I can tell you all about my product". Show the benefit to the customer!! The term consulting is very value added.

When I was a sales manager for a plastic housewares company, I offered, at no charge for my expertise, a service called Custom Kitchen Planning. I went into kitchens and mapped out exactly which products would fit in the individual's cupboards for specific items. The products saved a lot of space by grouping items together and saved money by keeping the food fresh. Some people shied away from this free service because they knew they would have to pay for the products, which was a sizeable investment. They also thought that in addition they would be paying me a large hourly fee. But, when I let them know I had "no-fee consulting," they were very eager to have me come over. These customers became some of my very best referrals. They saw that I really cared about them.

Using the word "free" when referring to your time, puts little or no value on you and your time. The terms "complimentary" or "no-fee" are more value-enhanced. And, your time is actually your most valuable commodity. People will appreciate your consulting more.

Copy Shops

As you implement the ideas in this book, you'll be making a few trips to the local copy shop to do photocopying. I've found that the locally-owned shops love to have a display of their customers' flyers. So, whatever you copy to promote your business, hang up a copy for the public to see, and check out the other flyers that are there!

Also see: advertising, business card flyers, bulletin boards

Corporate Gift Giving

Many companies spend a lot of money on gifts for their employees and/or customers. Specialty companies have catalogs that are full of gifts for appreciation and incentives. Why don't you create a Corporate Gift Giving Campaign with local companies. People like to deal with people they know. Start with companies that you do business with. A TWIST might be to talk to sales leaders of other direct-selling companies. Look inside the direct selling industry first. If your product is makeup, award your consultants with products from another company, like rubber stamps for use in their business, books, tapes, etc. The company you buy from can then give their sales force makeup.

Most businesses do not want to pay the retail markup. Check with your company to see if there is already a corporate plan in place; if not, suggest one. In any case, you might have to give up some of your profit, but the volume of sales will more than make up for it.

Baskets and sets of products are very popular for gift giving. You can customize your product to fit a specific business need. **Gift certificates are another popular alternative.**

I know of a sales consultant who was number one nationwide in her company because she showed the local bank how to use her product as an incentive for people opening new accounts. Change your TWIST a lot on this subject; you'll see very lucrative results!

Check for the **possibility of bartering** in full or in part.

Also see: bartering, cross-promoting

Correspondence

We live in a high-tech society. We communicate through satellites, e-mail, faxes, and telephones. This technology is a real boon to efficient business building. However, people still like the personal touch.

So, when you do correspond through "snail mail", **always include your business card and a little trinket.** My favorite trinkets are thought-provoking statements that are printed on nice card stock or stationery. This is a little bonus item I like to put in all my mail in addition to the note or letter I planned on sending originally.

Also see: mementos

Coupons

Create a coupon to encourage someone to try out your product/service. I like to do money off the purchase of a certain dollar amount. An idea that worked for me was to give a coupon worth $5 off the purchase of $25 regularly-priced merchandise.

Coupons are a wonderful idea if you're going door-to-door, participating in shows and events, or just to give out as a "complimentary gift" when you meet someone.

If you have a free seminar planned, have coupons for free tickets available to hand out. Stipulate that they must call ahead to get the tickets. This way you'll know how many to expect to attend.

Design of coupon: Use some of the great software programs available. Don't hand write the coupon; keep the look very professional. Some software has templates just for coupons. Use an expiration date. The closer the date, the sooner they'll have to use it. Print on a brightly-colored, heavier paper stock. The size should be a bit irregular so that the coupon doesn't get mixed in with everything else that is "standard" sized.

Distribution of coupon: You could use this in conjunction with many of the ideas in this book. Depending on the cost of your catalog and literature, you might attach one of these pieces to the coupon. After all, when your customers have a picture of what you have to offer, they'll be more inclined to redeem the coupon.
Make the buying process as easy as possible, with few strings attached.

What if someone calls you and the expiration date on the coupon has passed? Tell them you have a current coupon you can give them, rather than extending what they have. This way, you are creating urgency to place the order now! Always keep current coupons circulating.

When you hand out your coupons, attach your business card to it and vice versa.

Also see: business cards, door-to-door, events, grocery stores, parks, parking lots, seminars, tickets

Cross-promotion

This morning I made a plane reservation with American Airlines. After the agent gave me my confirmation number and our transaction was complete, she said that she could now transfer me to Hertz so I could rent a car at my destination. My husband was meeting me at the airport, so I didn't need that service. But, what if I would have needed a rental car? I could have made that reservation in the same phone call. This is an example of cross-promoting products. Two companies that complement, not compete with, each other.

How can you cross promote? Think of a product, company, or another business that will be enhanced by your product. For example, if you represent a grocery shopping service, your customers probably will be overstocked with groceries. They might need more storage containers, or they might need a new pantry built. Contact companies who sell or represent these products.
Do you sell children's books? Cross promote with someone who owns a preschool or day care.

Make arrangements to give coupons or other offers to your associate's customers. Sharing customer bases could also be beneficial, depending on your business arrangements. Be creative in finding and approaching cross promotion associates. In my book you'll notice I refer to The Booster, which is owned by Jenny Bywater. At my seminars, I tell the attendees to call her and purchase a catalog (1.800.5JENNYB). She has products that literally boost your sales. Her products range from postcards, to stickers, to buttons, and more. They give recognition and appreciation to both hostesses and consultants. I realized that her products and ideas complimented the information I teach at seminars. So, now we do seminars together and promote each other's products. We are able to share customers because people like you, who read my books and attend my seminars, see the value in using motivational products from the Booster.

MY OWN LEAD-GENERATING IDEAS:

D

Day Care Providers

People who care for children have a hard time getting out to do shopping. Take your product TO them. This is a great audience for anything relating to children, food, nutrition, and saving time.

These providers are great recruiting prospects. Many of them love what they do; however, some of the providers do this because they don't want to be out in the working world leaving their children, yet they need the income. You can give them another option to staying at home and earning a great income.

Where do you find these people? Look for ads in local papers, bulletin boards, and ask people you know who use the service of day care professionals. Call the department in your state which is responsible for the licensing of these providers and request a list.

Also see: bulletin boards, newspapers

Day Care Centers

If your product/service caters to children and their parents, you have a great target audience. Both you and the owner of the center can benefit when business is generated through referrals from the center because you can give useful, desirable products as an exchange.

Let's say that you sell toys through a demonstration plan. Talk to the owner of the center, and agree to have a display of your products and literature. **Schedule a week that you could personally be at the center** to meet parents as they are bringing their children in or taking them home. Decide on a time period, usually no more than two weeks, that **all the sales and new demonstrations generated from the parents would give the owner credit toward toys.** Award her as if she had a demonstration. Encourage her to get additional orders from people away from the day care center as well. This idea is not just for toys. It will work for any child/parent-related item.

Remember that parents are usually in a rush and won't have a lot of time to visit with you. You can incorporate a drawing so that you get their name and phone number. Also, encourage parents to take the catalogs to their work, family, and neighborhoods to gather orders. Award the parent getting the most orders/largest amount of sales some of your products.   An important key is to let parents know credit from the sales will go toward providing new toys for the center which will benefit *their* children. Everyone can be a winner here: the parents, the children, the owner, and you!

A *TWIST* on a full display is to feature only one of your key products.   In a situation where the customers don't have a lot of time to spend looking at what you have, this works great.   Promote that one item to the parents and then give free merchandise to the owner according to the amount of sales.

If the center has a newsletter, put regular notices in about you and your products.   Rather than just an advertisement, look into the possibility of **doing your own column in the newsletter** where you'll share pertinent ideas and information with the parents.

Hanging a poster or flyer in the center also works. You can give the owner your product in exchange for allowing you to promote your business in these ways. The more the owners have your product for use for the children, the more the children want, the more the parents buy.

As always, the goal here is to get new leads. I've had some day care displays where the sales were not so great, but I was able to service the parents, who in turn scheduled demonstrations with me, which resulted in more sales, customers, and profits.

Also see: coupons, drawings, flyers, fund raisers

Delivery People

Have you ever had anything delivered to your home--packages, furniture, pizza? Do a TWIST and **give the delivery person your sales literature and/or samples of your product.** Get their home phone and name so you can contact them during their personal time.

Also see: samples, literature

Dentist Offices

Also see: waiting rooms

Distance Customers

Thanks to technology, you can do business all over the country, and in many cases the world!! Shipping products is very cost-effective today. Think of all the people you know who don't live near you. Perhaps in other states, or cities. Don't think that you can't do business with them!

When you move. This is my area of expertise because of all the experience I have had! I keep the names of key customers and hostesses from my previous areas. This way they can place phone orders, and when you're back in the area, you can schedule several demonstrations to personally service them. Direct selling is relationship selling; keep the relationships going--even if you or your customers move!

Make a video of your demonstration. If you sell your product on a demonstration plan, this is a great idea!! You make either a personalized or a generic video and send to former customers (those who have moved or those where you used to live). People love this because it is unique and fun. They invite their friends as if you were having a live demonstration.

Because I have lived around the country, I have a lot of contacts. Twice a year, my company had really big challenge weeks. Obviously, I couldn't fly around the country to service my distance customers, so I created a video of my demonstration and mailed it out. My distant friend/relative would invite everyone to her home as if I were going to be there in person (in other words, the video viewing needs to be scheduled!). In the video package, I included all the catalogs, order forms, etc. that the hostess would need. (A return envelope for the orders and payments was also helpful.) This video turned out to be a real hit. Many of those in attendance already knew me, so they had fun watching. One time, my mother-in-law video taped the demonstration on her end and mailed it back to me with the orders. Not only did this help to promote my big week, but also everyone had a lot of fun!!

Get orders from as many states as possible. Get names from your Christmas card list, school alumni directory, former customers who have moved to other states, relatives, etc. Let them know your goal of getting orders from every state in the country. Ask your friends for referrals. This is a fun challenge to do in celebration of the 4th of July or Labor day. It needs to be planned in advance for maximum results. In the packet of information you send, list the states you don't know anyone in and ask your primary list for referrals. You'll be surprised at how your incremental sales will snowball!

Displays

Put a **box with an advertisement** about your business on the counters of businesses you frequent. Good choices are video stores, beauty shops, cleaners, copy shops, tanning salons, and so forth. Every time you walk into a place of business, consider talking to the owner about this idea.

You can make your own box or purchase a display-style box at a local paper supplier. **The box display could include flyers, coupon offers, product literature, and business cards.** The key is to get the names and phone numbers of those who want to do business with you. Remember, people rarely call you, even if they want your product. Have a local printer supply you with note pads printed with spaces for name, phone, and address. Attach these pads to the box and provide a place for them to be deposited in the box. Do a drawing for products. Gather these leads often. Offer the business owner free products and referrals in exchange for letting you use some counter space.

One sales leader shared her experience when she saw a display box from her company at the local beauty salon. She asked the stylist the name of the representative who had the display box. The stylist said, "Oh, please give me that box. The lady hasn't been back for weeks, I'm going to throw it away." This smart leader told the stylist that she would take care of the box. Upon opening it, she found twelve leads. When she called the people, nine wanted to buy or sell her product. The moral is to maintain your display boxes by checking on them weekly and letting the owners/employees of the business know the box is valuable to you--it is!!

Also see: cross promotion, displays, vendors

Doctor Offices

Also see: waiting rooms

Donations

Many organizations do auctions for fund raisers. They are always looking for businesses to donate products/services. Offer what you can and ask that you get the name of the person who got your items so you can follow up with service.

Donations are also solicited for club drawings and prizes. If you have excess inventory, take the first step and go out to organizations and offer your products to be used promotionally or for raising funds.

Are you aware of organizations that can benefit from using your product? If you sell cellular phones, can you donate the phone and then the organization pays for the air time? Donations are normally tax deductible and help the recipients. Your benefit comes from giving the gift and then the possibility of receiving new business.

Door-to-Door, those you'd like to know

Have you ever driven through a neighborhood and thought that you'd like to do business with the residents? This is the beauty of a direct selling business. You can go **to** them.

When I had been in the industry just a few years, our family moved from a small town in Michigan to big-city Detroit. And I knew no one there! Going door-to-door was one method that I used consistently to build my business to be one of the top producing in the nation. This is easy and fun; you're meeting new friends as well as business contacts.

How you decide to go door-to-door is up to you. You can go by yourself, with one of your associates, (best if this person is one from your own team or organization so you can teach them while you work!), or if you have little kids and want to go for a walk put them in the stroller and go meet people in your community.

I like to dress according to the weather and not be too dressed up-- business/casual works. If you're in a business suit and heels, people think you're selling them something and are not as open to talk to you. On the other hand, you can dress casually and still be professional. If your company provides name tags, wear one so it can be seen immediately. This provides instant credibility.

Don't carry a suitcase full of stuff! I've found it is best to carry sales catalogs, recruiting literature, flyers showing current specials, and a coupon with an offer. If your company has small, inexpensive samples, bring these along for the more interested people. Magnets with your name will also be a boost. And, the most important items are a pad of paper and pen. If your company provides mailing lists in duplicate, these also help. But remember, the pen and something to write on are the most crucial.

Decide what your purpose is in meeting these new customers. Do you want to sell product, recruit, schedule demonstrations, or all of the above. All of the above is the right answer, but my first goal is to find people who want to attend a presentation of my product. From there, I can lead them into buying, hosting, and recruiting. When you go to the door, **your biggest asset is your smile!!!** As soon as they answer, let them be immediately attracted to you. Here's an idea of what to say:

"Hi, I'm Christie with _____(with your name tag on, they'll know for sure this is who you are!). I'm not selling anything today......(they're thinking "whew", I'll listen now). I'm in the neighborhood providing new catalogs of our products. Would you like one? (if they don't want one, don't make them take one!). I'm going to be holding a demonstration of our products in your neighborhood, **would you like to attend?** (this is real low-key-- you're not asking for any big commitments).
A lot of different things can happen. They might say NO to everything you ask; no big deal, thank them for their time, give them another smile and go on.

If they do want some literature about your product, they are more likely to say "yes" to attending a demonstration. They are going to ask you, "when is the demonstration?" You tell them that you haven't decided on the time and place, but get their name and phone number so you can call and let them know. Most people are really open to this option if they are interested in your product.

Then, **ask her who in the neighborhood is the "party person"**-- the person who loves to entertain and have the neighbors over or who has hosted product demonstrations in the past. If there is such a person in the neighborhood, they'll tell you right away! Thank her for her time and assure her that you'll be in contact. You'll go to the party person's home last. Go to the next house and repeat the scenario.

The idea is to compile a guest list of all the people who want to attend a demonstration of your product. When you get to the party person's home, let her know that all these neighbors want to come to a demonstration, you're just looking for someone who would like the gifts! If you've made double or triplicate copies of the names, addresses, and phones, you can leave one with the person who has
scheduled a demonstration, and you'll have one as well.

Now, what if you don't get a party person referral? That's okay. Just keep going around the neighborhood; you'll meet someone who you would love to have a demonstration with. Tell her that all the people on the list want to attend a demonstration, and you're just looking for someone to give the gifts to. This is a very, very effective way of gaining new customers. More people would schedule product demonstrations if they knew who to invite and if those people would come. If you hand a list of already-invited people to a potential hostess, she'll be very likely to say YES!

When you meet your next hostesses, plan her demonstration as you normally would. Encourage her to invite more people, particularly outside of the neighborhood. The key in any demonstration planning is to find what she wants to get for having the demonstration and then showing her how to get it!

You don't have to wait for the last person before setting up a demonstration. When I first came up with this approach (out of necessity because I had no demonstrations scheduled), I actually chose the first person I talked with to have a demonstration. Then, I just reversed the process. We scheduled the date and time; as I walked around the neighborhood, I invited the neighbors for her. She followed through with a reminder call and also invited people from outside of her area. She had a great demonstration, and by the way, the demonstration was held within five days of being scheduled--the closer the better!!

What if no one wants to host a demonstration? Hold on to that list!! You can invite them to a demonstration that you'll be holding in their area or in your own home. If nothing else, call the people back who you gave literature to. Ask them for their order.

How do you decide which neighborhoods to go to? Pick homes that look friendly; decorated, doors open, cars around, kid's bikes, swing sets. Compliment them on their home! As you work in your city, you'll also know who is moving in and out. Make a point to meet the newcomers.

Also see: new neighbors

Drawings

See: cross promoting, displays, events

Drive-through windows

Everyone likes surprises; even people who work in businesses with drive-through windows. When you drive through and hand these people your payments, give them a surprise--your sales and recruiting literature. These people make great recruit prospects; they typically have low wages and are eager for new challenges. Remember to get their names, addresses, and phone number!

MY OWN LEAD-GENERATING IDEAS:

E

Easter

Holidays are always a fun time to celebrate. Purchase the plastic u-fill-em eggs. Put notes on the inside of each with special offers, like the following:
1. free shipping
2. coupon for $5 off $25 purchase
3. free product

During the holiday season, carry around a basket with these eggs in it everywhere you go--a real attention getter!! When you meet someone you want to do business with, have them choose an egg. Put some wrapped Easter candy inside each egg as well. This adds more value. Even if the people don't do business with you immediately, they won't forget you as being a fun, festive, service person (be sure to get their NAPEF and give them your business card).

E-mail

To find new customers: Post your product/service on the news service of bulletin boards.

People finder: Most web browsers have services where you can find people.. While spamming (sending massive amounts of junk mail via e-mail) is forbidden, you can hand pick people through the people finders. You can target a last name, a city, etc. Send them a **personalized** e-mail message.

I consult with a direct selling company whose product is grocery shopping information via the Internet. Doing cold calling out of the phone book isn't effective because subscribers to this service need to be connected to the Internet. Usually people who have the Internet use it for many facets of their lives. So, using the People

Finder has worked really well for them. If you have a product with a similar target audience, this would be a good method.

Elevators

Have you noticed how people act in an elevator? They walk in, press the button for their floor, and stare at the door. You could have a wonderful captive audience here. Just ask, "would you like something to read while you're waiting to arrive at your floor?" Give them some literature or business card, whatever you feel is suitable for this situation. If nothing else, the ice is broken, and the ride is more enjoyable!!!! Get names and phones of those who are receptive.

Events

This is becoming a very popular way to get new business leads. In fact, after one of my cross-country moves, I participated in a holiday craft fair event in my new area. The leads I got from that one event were the catapult for huge business growth. I did business with many of those people for years and years. Through the years I've exhibited in events from small, rural county fairs to huge metro events. Some common denominators for success in all events are listed here.

Choosing an event. Pick one that will bring a target audience to you. If you sell kitchen ware, going to a gun show will not be the best idea. However, a home and garden show or family fair would work rather well. Companies selling makeup do well at women's fairs and so on.

Placement of booth.   Ask to be scheduled away from your competitors as well as away from others selling your same product. This is so that the visitors to your booth do not confuse you with someone else. Try to get a high-traffic area; sometimes the cost is higher; you'll have to determine if it is worth it.

Share a booth. Booths can be costly, depending on many factors. Events can run from one to ten days. Therefore, sharing a booth with other consultants in you company makes a lot of sense because you can share the time slots and cost.

Distributing leads. If more than one consultant is working at a booth at the same time, have your drawing slips printed up in different colors of paper. Or, stamp your name on the backs of the drawing slips that you will use. When you share like this, the most common method of distributing leads and sales is whoever talks to the customer has that customer as a lead/customer. Once in a while, I've known of people who come back to the booth on a different day, and not knowing this policy, give their name to a second consultant. So, in that case, **lead goes to the first to follow through.** Situations always seem to arise, so try to work out a policy in advance and then be professional and work toward a win/win. Many times you'll get leads from opposite ends of the state/city that you might not want. Make an agreement with someone in those areas to trade leads.

The Set up. Keep everything professional looking. Do not use handwritten signs. See if your company has signs or logos that you can use. Remember, at an event you are in direct comparison with other companies, so look your best in all ways.

Open vs. closed booths. Make your booth inviting as if customers were coming into your store. My suggestion is a "U Shape" configuration. This way you have three times more table space than if you put on table across the booth. Remember, you are paying for space; use it wisely! Many booths have the displays behind the consultants, and the consultants at a table essentially blocking access to the booth. Potential customers don't get to see the products very well, and the aisles get really crowded. You'll need to check the event contract to see what is and is not allowed.

The purpose of your participating in this event is to meet new customers/recruits. The problem is that so do the other one hundred plus exhibitors! Make your booth stand out. The attendees are going to be bombarded with pitches and literature from every booth they visit. Make yours different.

Be an active exhibitor. Many people just sit in their chairs, fold their arms, and some even have their noses in books waiting for people to come to their booth. The non-verbal message they send is not one of "welcome to my booth."

The key is to go out TO the people! Honorary days work great. When you see someone that you'd like to talk to, find something about them that you could honor and recognize. If you see someone you'd like to know who has red hair, walk up to her and say, "Congratulations, today is Red Hair day at _____(your company). Give them a little token gift; stickers or product literature (something with your name on it) to break the ice and have them want to come and visit your booth. Check your contracts to see if you have limits as to where you can stand; some contracts state that you must stay within your booth. If this is the case, all you need to do is project your voice so your visitor can hear you!

Put a dish of wrapped candy out to lure people to come over. **Music,** if allowed, or other multi-media attracts visitors as do **cooking demos** if any of these are appropriate to your company.

Drawing Forms. Your goal is to get names of new customers. You must have a way of asking for this information that is a real benefit to the prospect. Drawings work wonders. Most people know why you are doing this and are usually willing to fill out a slip. **Make the forms simple to fill out!** Don't ask a lot of complicated questions! A person should be able to fill out the slip in less than 60 seconds. Clipboards with pens attached are a necessity in a booth for this very purpose.

You can fill out the slips for a more personal touch. If your booth isn't really busy (I hope it is!), and you have the luxury of talking individually to each visitor, I have found that simply asking the visitor the questions on the slip and filling it out myself works very well. Why do I suggest this? So that you can get to know the people, and they are not just a name on a piece of paper. You can jot down notes about which products they are interested in, what concerns they have, what they were wearing, anything to help you remember them when you do a follow-up call. Also, attendees often have their arms full of stuff they've picked up from other booths, and trying to balance your form with all this is uncomfortable. In fact, many times they hurry through it so fast, they forget important items--like their phone numbers! Remember, in most cases, you are not going to be selling as much as you are looking for new business, hostesses, and recruits. The main idea is to find out who is interested or potentially interested.

Maybe they'll say that they'd love to have a demonstration with you when school is out. Write that down. All of a sudden, **you have warm leads.** I suggest that you **give them a sample of your product, a business card, or some small, inexpensive item that they'll want to keep to remember you by**.

Be prepared for those ready to buy or sign up. You might have someone so thrilled to meet you and see your product/service that they are ready to sign up or buy on the spot! Be prepared for this as well. Don't make them wait to get going! This means having literature/products for ordering, holding demonstrations, and recruiting. You probably will still have some follow through to do. FOLLOW THROUGH AND THROUGH AND YOU'LL NEVER BE THROUGH!

You'll also want to have an **exclusive offer for your booth visitors.** Coupons work, or if you carry inventory, bring some along and offer at a cash and carry price--especially if the items are no longer available, or if you're overstocked.. Just because someone doesn't want your product that very day doesn't mean they won't have interest or a referral when you call them back. I've found that people don't like lugging products around the events, so they actually prefer to be contacted later.

Many companies have a **grand prize drawing with one winner,** and then the rest of the people are considered runners-up and are given an offer when you call them back. Even if all consultants combined their resources to give one big item away, I still prefer to have my own Grand Prize Drawing. The **runner-up prize** is very effective as well. I've made many loyal customers beginning with this approach.

Be **prepared for sales, scheduling demonstrations,** and answering questions about joining the company. Some people are ready on the spot; accommodate them.

The most important key to any business is the follow through!! You can have the best-looking booth, get hundreds of leads, but nothing, absolutely nothing works until you follow through! Remember this: **Follow through and you'll never be through!**

Other exhibitors. Get to know the other folks who have booths. Use the ideas you're reading in this book to do cross-promoting and reverse selling.

Also see: coupons, drawings

Exhibits

See: events

MY LEAD-GENERATING IDEAS:

F

Family

You're saying, "I already talked to all my family members; that's why I'm reading this book; I want to expand beyond my family." You're right. However, (get ready for another *TWIST*), if you really have talked to all your blood relatives--all of them--move to the next level.

What about **in-laws of your siblings, spouse, children, cousins,** etc. What about the cousins of your cousins (those not on your side). Contact the family of your family and then the family of those family members. If you did this on ALL your family as well as your customers, pretty soon (well, this would take a while), you'd contact the whole world because somewhere we are all related!

Fast Food Places

This is a great mom idea. Most fast food outlets have playgrounds. While the kids are playing, the moms (and dads) can network. To break the ice, carry your product bag complete with literature, samples, interest bags, and products, if appropriate.

This area also becomes a great mine for recruiting because families with young children have a great need for extra money and usually desire to work at home to avoid the hassles of child care.

Flyers

These can be relatively inexpensive, and can be used in a variety of ways. Keep a stack of flyers handy to give away wherever you go. Leave at businesses, give in place of business cards, hang up all over town!

Flyers are great for your own neighborhood because your neighbors know who you are; you're now letting them know that you can service them with your product. If you have little children, putting a flyer together and then taking a walk will help you meet new friends while entertaining your children. However, if the conversation gets involved and your children are restless, make an appointment for a return visit without the children.

If your children are older (pre-teen and teen) who want to earn money, hire them to deliver flyers and pay them per flyer delivered with a bonus attached when the people they deliver to do business with you.

Make the flyers easy to read, don't put in a lot of words. Use a brightly colored paper, perhaps an odd size as well. The headline will be the main event here, make them responsive; give prospects a reason to call you right away!

Also see: grocery stores, business card flyers, neighborhoods, cars, parking lots, bulletin boards, headlines.

Follow Through

I hope you don't skip through this very important step. Once you have met someone, got their NAPEF, and want to do business, this is just the beginning. This is just planting the seed. The follow through comes from phone calls, notes, and fulfilling any promises made (sending a catalog, taking care of items that need service, etc.)
In the next Lemon Aid book, I'll give you tips on nurturing the seeds. In the meantime, **Follow through with your customers and you'll never be through with your business.**

Fund Raisers

Many direct sales companies offer programs for raising funds. If yours does not, make up your own by giving a percentage of your profit to the organization. This is really helpful when you do speaking engagements to non-profit groups to educate them about the field of interest that includes your product. While this wouldn't necessarily be a selling event, you could tell them that whatever they order or whatever orders they bring to you in a certain amount of time, you'll give some of the profit to the group. You could offer an incentive for the person who gets the most orders.

If you are doing a full-blown fund raiser, much more organization and detail are involved. Every detail needs to be planned out to make the event most profitable for you and the group.

Here are some general, helpful steps to successful fund raisers:

1. Have the organization decide on a goal--how much do they want to earn? What will the money be used for?

2. How much needs to be sold to meet this goal? How many average-size orders will be needed to sell this much product? Now both you and the organization have goals clearly defined.

3. How will the fund raiser be promoted? Will you do a demonstration of the products or just have people collect orders? Whichever way you choose, an announcement meeting to the general group is beneficial--if not critical--to the success of the fund raiser.

4. Will you give incentives? Who will provide them? What will the incentives be given for? Highest sales? Most orders? Whenever possible, use your product as an incentive to get more and bigger orders.

5. Include a letter of explanation to those who will be gathering orders. Make this letter simple! Instruct the order collectors to get everyone's NAPEF.

6. Make the event simple, get the NAPEF, grow extra business!

How do you find fund raisers?

1. **Support as many fund raisers** as you possibly can when people approach you; this becomes a form of reverse selling.

2. **Be aware of fund raisers that are going on around you** as you are out and about. This way, after you have purchased their product, ask how much money they have made. Then tell them how you can do a fund raiser with your product/service. The

general public gets tired of buying candy and non-useful gift items to help these organizations. Your product could be the answer to their money problems.

Also See: Car washes, bake sales

Former Business Associates

Think of people you know from where you used to work or who used to work where you do. Contact them; let them know about your new business. Perhaps they are looking for a company to be involved with--great recruiting potential!   If they don't need or want what you have to offer, ask for referrals.

Former Customers

Have you owned a business before your present one? Have you worked in a previous job where you were able to service people who remember your outstanding service? This should be one of the first groups of people you contact! You have already shown them what a wonderful person you are to work with. In cases like this, products and opportunities are secondary to the relationship you have already established. When you contact these former customers, your name alone is all the clout you'll need to win their business and loyalty once again. Call these people immediately; your reputation will certainly precede you!

What about people who used to work with your present company, and for some reason, chose to give up their business. Contact their former customers. These people are already golden nuggets because they are familiar, and probably love, your product and plan. How do you get the names and information? **Offer to purchase the previous consultant's business.** This is an offer most people leaving a business won't refuse.

I gave away my customer list a couple of times--definitely not a good idea--and then learned how to sell the good will that I built up through the years. I have purchased and sold customer lists two ways.

The first idea is when you want to **buy the business of someone leaving the business**. Most people leave because they run out of business--they didn't have the privilege of reading this book!! However, I am convinced that no one would run out of customers if they really served them. Those customers would continually buy or recruit, and then they would tell more people about you. So, be sure the business you buy is really *good* business. Do this on a percentage basis. Offer to pay the person who is quitting 10 to 20 percent of the sales that you *initially* generate from their customers. The percentage you offer will be based on the commissionable profit you get from the company. If your commission is 25%, I'd only give 10%. However, if you earn 50%, give 20%. These are just some guidelines. Keep track of the *first-time business* that you generate. If you contact Christopher Miller and he buys $50 of your products, you'd owe the selling consultant a percentage of the $50. However, when Christopher buys the next $50, you don't owe the previous consultant anything; you're the one who generated that next level of sales. Keep good records and be honest in paying the seller. This is a three-way, win-win situation because all parties involved benefit.

The next situation is **when you need to sell some of your customer base** because you have too much business to handle (what a nice problem), you're moving away from your customers and feel they need a local service person (my case), or you are leaving the business for something more lucrative (not because you ran out of customers!!). In my case, I sold products through the demonstration plan. I had a file folder for every hostess that ever held a demonstration. In the folder were orders from anyone who ever placed an order from the demonstrations. I had hundreds of file folders at one time and was relocating. I bundled up the folders and sold as a sets. I made over $1,000. Keep in mind that the people who bought the business from me knew I was the best consultant and gave superb service--they knew the business was good; they were excited to be able to actually buy leads instead of having to drum them up themselves. And, I felt better as I left the area because I knew my customers were being taken care of.

The next move I made was when I sold a franchise of the business, and the new owners were contractually entitled to all demonstration records. As I was preparing to vacate the building, I left boxes and boxes of these. When I came back to get more of my belongings, the new owner asked me to take the boxes with me; he didn't want them!! I couldn't believe his thinking!! Those records *were* the business he was paying for!! The boxes were full of customers who already knew and loved the product! I was leaving the area, or I would have gladly taken them. The next time I went back to the office the boxes were gone. Hopefully they weren't thrown out but were used for building a business--the real reason records should be kept!

Winning new customers takes much more time, energy, and money than keeping and nurturing those you already do business with. Yet, most consultants spend most of the time only on new business development. Obviously, you must always have the new; but don't forget the old. I am reminded of a poem:

Make new friends, but keep the old.
One is silver, the other is gold.

I believe the same can be said for customers and recruits.

MY OWN LEAD-GENERATING IDEAS:

G

Garage Sales

You're probably thinking how much work is involved in a garage sale and how this idea isn't going to work for you. Remember the *TWIST?* This idea doesn't mean holding your own; the idea is to go to garage sales and meet the people who are holding them!!

You can find out a lot about people by seeing what kinds of things they are getting rid of. Let's say you sell home decorating items. As you're browsing through the sale items ask the person a question something like this: "I see you're getting rid of a lot of your pictures; are you redecorating?" ("yes" is the most likely answer). You reply, "You are so lucky that I stopped by, my specialty is home decor and I have a free catalog for you. After your garage sale is over, may I stop by and offer my no-fee consulting service?" What if she has already redecorated? No problem, she may need accent pieces. Most people are so impressed that you NOTICE something about THEM, that they are very open to doing business with you. Keep a stack of sales/recruiting literature handy and ask permission to leave them near the check out area. Tell her if she gets the names and phone numbers of the people who take your catalog, you'll give her a bonus based on how much business you generate from her leads. Make getting the leads easy for her by supplying a tear pad for people to write their names, addresses, and phone numbers.

This next idea takes some advanced planning and is very worthwhile. Read the paper for the garage sale listings. Call and set up this type of referral/bonus network ahead of time. This way, you can take a display box along. Who knows, this person might enjoy giving you referrals so much that she'll be your next recruit!

Many times garage sales will be sponsored by groups wanting to raise money. Not only can you see if they'll help distribute catalogs, but you can also **offer them the opportunity to have a fund raiser with you.**

Even though it requires a lot of work, **holding your own garage**

sale is a great way of meeting new customers. I always kept the newest products from my company in my own home; consequently, I had older, perfectly good, products that I didn't use and was very willing to sell at a garage sale. Without fail, I met many new people who became my customers because they first bought these products at my garage sale. Just as you would ask a person holding a garage sale to get names and phones of those who pick up a catalog, you'll want to get the names of those coming to your own garage sale.

Do a drawing and give away a huge bag of items instead of selling them (or, do several drawings throughout the day.) Trust me, everyone who visits your sale will want to win this surprise bag; they will gladly give you their NAPEF! Again we see the beauty of direct selling; you're able to promote your business while engaging in a non-business activity!

Also see fund raisers, displays

Grocery Stores

Do you love to go grocery shopping? Most of us don't. Did you know that **you can gather leads and build your business while you're at the grocery store?** This idea can be used for any product/service; however, if you sell something that can be related or linked to grocery store items, this is a real gold mine because you'll be working with a target audience (i.e. your product is kitchen utensils, plastic housewares, grocery coupons, or other items that complement food purchases). This is one of my favorite methods, so I am listing several ideas here. Don't feel like you have to use them all at the same time--you'd be in the store for hours!

Wear your name tag *if you're dressed to do business.* If I am out visiting clients or conducting other business, I usually have my name tag on anyway. If you're in your normal clothes, don't do this. As I show you this lead-generation technique, it is very low-key and natural. So, sometimes if you're not dressed for business, you'll have more success. However, if you haven't combed your hair, brushed your teeth, or put on deodorant, don't go lead hunting--I've had to do emergency grocery runs looking like this before; I always hoped that I'd never run into any one I knew let alone be an advertisement (and a poor one at that) for my business!

Badges with cleaver sayings attract attention. A grocery store is a great place to wear these!

The parking lot: When you get out of your car, be prepared with simple flyers. On this flyer, have an attention-getting, direct-response headline. Most direct sellers will go put these on all the windshields of all the cars in the parking lots. Please don't do this. In many places this is forbidden because the flyers blow all over and create unsightly litter. However, leaving a message on two, three, four, or five cars shouldn't matter. Put the flyers on both of the cars parked directly next to you, and then the three cars that face these. This takes just seconds to do. If you have some kind of a sample, this is a great time to give it away; people will feel like they were worth more than a piece of paper. A valuable, close-expiration coupon or offer could also work. Remember, you want them to respond because you don't have their NAPEF--yet.

Another idea along the same lines: **have an offer printed up on cards the size of business cards.** You can put this either on the windshield or on the handle of the door. This is smaller and less bulky. People collect business cards and could be more inclined to read and keep something on this format.

Product/Shopping Bag. Does you company have its own shopping bags? You know, bags with the company name and logo on it that you put customers' purchases in? These bags make terrific shopping bags! I've seen nice bags complete with handles, plastic grocery shopping bags with company's logo on, and plain bags with nothing written on them. If your company's bag falls under the latter category, just decorate the plain bag by cutting out pictures, logos, and type from catalogs and other literature. The idea is for people to see your bag!! I suggest using a bag like this in place of a purse or wallet. Put your wallet, checkbook, and shopping list inside and go shopping!

The Foyer. This is the part of the store that has the Community Bulletin Board. Be prepared to hang up a Business-Card Flyer. Keep a supply of thumb tacks, tape, and stapler in your purse/briefcase/product bag so you'll have the tools to hang the flyer up. While you're hanging the flyer, take a minute to look at those who are already posted. Remember, use the Reverse Selling technique. **Who on the board has a business or service that could benefit from your business/service?** Anyone you'd like to barter with? How about possible cross-promotions. Always, always, always read the bulletin boards to get new leads.

Now you're in the store. You have your grocery shopping cart and are ready to shop. **Put your grocery list on a clipboard with an attention-getting flyer attached to the back side of the clipboard**. This way, as you're holding your list to shop, other shoppers will see the flyer with your attention-getting headline. Under your list, have a sheet where you can record NAPEFs, and place your stacks of flyers underneath this sheet so that you can hand them out as you meet prospects. Keep in mind that this is a very low-key approach; you are gathering leads while you're doing a personal activity--grocery shopping. If you have something that piques someone's interest, they'll stop you and ask you, and you want to be prepared. One company that I consult with on selling grocery shopping information uses this often. The catchy headline for people to see is simply "Do you buy groceries?" The grocery store is the perfect place for this question! When people stop you and answer your attention-getting question or inquire about your product, you'll be equipped with something to give them as well as getting their NAPEF.

Children in Shopping Carts and Crying Children. We've all seen these kids, heard them, or even raised them! Having your child scream because he/she wants something can be rather embarrassing! This method allows you to help the mom or dad console the child, and let's you meet new customers. The concept is to **give the child a safe, little gift to divert his/her attention and calm him down.** Attached to the gift is your business card, coupon, or a catchy advertisement about joining your company as a gift for the parent. Believe me, the parent will remember you and listen to you!

If your product is targeted at children, perhaps your company provides you with some small give always. If not, I use items purchased at the dollar store, or better yet, toys that come in the boxes of cereal or from the kids' meals at fast food places and write my own advertisement.

Recently, I had some plastic toy airplanes. On some card stock, I wrote, "Talk to me about a prepaid vacation with your family."

Nothing super creative, but people do pay attention, and they remember you!! As you're talking to the parent, remember the all important NAPEF!!

Incremental lead gathering: While you're shopping, observe other shoppers. Look at them and ask yourself, "What can I offer this person to make her life better, easier, safer?" This would be whatever benefit you have to offer through your product/service.

Let's pretend for a moment. You sell scrapbooks and supplies and notice a mom with young kids struggling to keep the kids in the cart and in her view. Always start with a sincere compliment to open the conversation such as "Your kids are adorable, how old are they?" Moms always love a break to talk to an adult and will answer your question plus add more information (in most cases). As you go through this rather quick, informal conversation, add something similar to this, "I've discovered a way to preserve the memories of my family, are you interested in scrapbooking? I just happen to have a sale flyer that you can have; it includes a _____(mention offer) coupon. Would you like one?" Be sure that you get the NAPEF.

If you sell rubber stamp supplies and see someone looking at the card section, casually ask if they love having to spend time and money looking for cards. Most people do not. Let them know you can teach them how to create their own. The object here is not to discourage her from buying a product in the store--that's not being a good business neighbor--but rather to get her thinking about what you can offer her aside from what she is purchasing.

Lines. The most dreaded part of the shopping experience can become very profitable in the way of meeting new people when you're standing in line. I always seem to have more items than the express line will allow, but as you'll now see, you want to be in a lengthy line so you can linger longer and meet leads.

Observe the people around you and what they are buying. If you see a man buying stacks of frozen dinners, you MIGHT surmise (but do not assume!) that he is single. You could open the conversation with a complimentary statement and lead in with questions.

Try this: "Looks like you're a great cook!" Depending on his response is how you'll take the conversation. Some people are tight-lipped and don't want to visit with anyone. Respect this type of person. However, I 've found that most people like to while away the line-standing time and will open up. He might say, "My wife is out of town this week". Well, now you know that he isn't single. If your product is nutritional supplements, this is a great way to briefly tell what you do and what you market. I always tell people, "this is your lucky day, (every time someone meets me, they're lucky; and I'm lucky for having met them as well!) I just discovered some nutritional supplements that will add value to the foods you already eat."

If you are a female, males sometimes shy away. If you know they are married, (or you can outright ask if they are), ask for his wife's name. And, if you're male, this works by asking a woman for her husband's name. Spouses always seem willing to give their partner's name out.

You might have heard me speak about how I got started in the direct selling industry. If not, you and your company should contact me. After hearing my story, you'll know why I recommend that you watch for women who are buying twinkies or women's magazines; especially soap opera magazines. These women are great recruiting possibilities; they could become the tops of the top!

Cashiers. Once you've made your way to the checkstand, you now have a new prospect, the cashier! In most cases, they'll say something trite like,"Hi, how are you today?" Respond by using their name (look at the name tag). "I'm wonderful, Amy (use the right name), how are you doing?" A person's name is the sweetest word to them. Get to know the checker in much the same way as I've suggested that you talk with customers.

Ask questions about them! As you talk to the cashier, you'll see ways that your business/product can be of benefit. This is a great recruiting opportunity as I have found many checkers don't relish standing on their feet all day. So, I say something like, "Amy, you must really like your job here (always assume that she/he does!). Usually the response is negative. Weave your commercial into your conversation. After I pay for my groceries (do remember to pay; I've gotten so caught up in interesting conversations, that I've forgotten to pay!), I thank the cashier for the great service and say, "I have a gift for you." The gift can be your catalog or other literature. Just be sure to get the NAPEF for follow through!

Gifts

Whenever any gift-giving occasion arises, think of your product first as an appropriate gift. Not only can you give a nicer gift because you buy the product at wholesale cost, but the recipient becomes acquainted with your product. Include your business card as well as a catalog with the gift so the recipient can order more. This is also helpful information if an exchange needs to be made.

Teachers. One of my friends swears that the way her kids got good grades is because she gave their school teachers products from her business for every holiday and other gift-giving occasions! This is a thoughtful gesture and also expands your business because other teachers see the gift ideas and will want to purchase items from you. They also identify you with your product line, and this is also a great way to introduce your product as a potential fund raiser.

Corporations spend thousands of dollars on gifts for their employees, vendors, and customers. How could you promote your product to be their gift-of-choice? While these companies are usually conscious of price, the service is what will make the biggest difference to them. Let them know that you can serve them. If you can give a corporate or volume discount, you may be able to secure the business even easier.

Advertise this service by having a separate business card printed that says "I specialize in corporate gift giving." When you meet people on a professional level, give them this card rather than your regular one.

Gift Certificates

Offer gift certificates as a gift-giving alternative to your customers who are perplexed about what to give someone else. The beauty of this is you'll easily attract new customers because the certificate must be purchased and redeemed through you. Be sure the certificate states this so the recipient doesn't get confused and go to another consultant. When you sell the certificate, ask the purchaser for the recipient's name and phone. This has helped me in many cases. People really get busy and forget they hold a gift certificate. Follow through on your part shows you are anxious for the recipient to enjoy their gift. Your business will flourish!

Gift Certificates work to show appreciation to those who service you. I've used them for servers in restaurants, hotel housekeeping staff, nice cashiers, and so on. Your business will grow because they **call you** to redeem their gift. When I issue this type of certificate, I put a close-dated expiration so that they'll take quick action! I've never had anyone purchase just the free amount (I usually give them $5 certificates); they've always used it toward a much larger purchase. Remember that this is just the beginning of a longer-term business relationship. You'll discover that by giving gift certificates, you're investing in new customers and cementing relationships.

MY LEAD-GENERATING IDEAS:

H

Handouts

Carry small, simple handouts to give to potential customers and recruits that will really get their attention. To a simple headline printed on colorful cardstock, I attach related inexpensive candy, items from a novelty shop or dollar store, or toys from cereal boxes and from kids meals from fast food places.

From a kids meal last week, I got a play passport promoting a new movie. My headline read, "Your passport to financial freedom--call me for details." I attached a small-sized Big Hunk candy bar and wrote, "You'll make a Big Hunk of money when you join my team!" The headlines are easy to come up with. Just look at the item and add your own TWIST. Remember to print your name and phone on the advertisement or attach a business card.

I keep these items in my product bag, purse, and/or briefcase. When I meet someone I'd like to work with, I give them this little gift.

Halloween

When the trick or treaters come to your door, in addition to handing out treats, give them some literature and/or samples of your product in their bag. Put your name and phone number on everything and add a coupon. A simple note saying, "A Treat for Mom (or Dad)" works very well. Of course, if you have a miniature size candy bar, the parents will be thrilled!

During the Halloween season, carry a treat bag or plastic pumpkin around filled with treats to give to potential customers. Tape your business card to the treat; exchange your treat for their NAPEF.

Headlines

When a potential customer reads any of your sales/recruiting literature, your goal is to have them respond quickly! If they have to muddle through pages of information, they put it aside until they have time. Using a very simple, catchy headline will encourage this quick response. If you're not skilled at thinking up these headlines, do a TWIST. Read and observe literature that you get from other businesses. How could you incorporate new ideas into your business? Read a lot of magazines, open your junk mail; they are full of ideas!

Here are some very simple ones I've seen and used.
"Don't Throw Me Away"
"Give me Away"
"Read This"
"Pass me On"
"Need _____?" (Money, Time, Energy, etc)
"Are you looking for_____?" (New job, happiness, peace,)
"Are you confused about_____?" (insurance, legal advice,)

Adapt these headlines to the needs of your customers and the benefits you can offer.

Home Shows

Most communities have either a parade of homes program where builders construct showcase homes in one neighborhood or scattered around the city and sell tickets to allow the public to tour these decorated houses. Additionally, some shows have an exhibit tent set up so prospects can meet vendors. Would you like to be one of these vendors? Usually the entrance fee is high and the event goes for over a week. You should consider sharing the booth cost and time slots with other consultants.

I prefer having a display in one of the homes. Contact your home builders association and find out when this event is held. Get names of participating builders and contact them. Ask if the home is a builder spec home or if someone has already purchased it. If the builder owns the home work with him. This can be a great opportunity for some cross promoting. Otherwise, contact the owners to make arrangements with them.

When I have done these, I have worked directly with the home owner. I was able to get the owner really excited about my product and showed her how the product would benefit her in her new home. I proposed a display to be set up in the home during the show. You can choose how long you will be on site--unlike being in the exhibit tent. Because the home show goes on for several days, I usually just set up a product display along with a drawing visitors can enter and a coupon they can take. On particularly busy days, like weekends, I would stay at the home to answer questions. Other than that, I would stop by daily to freshen up the display and gather the drawing slips.

After the home show was over, I scheduled a demonstration with the owner so she could show off the home to her friends and family, and I could educate and service them on my product and service. I gave the homeowner any credit for the referrals and sales I gained from the home show display. If she chose not to have a demonstration, I gave her referral credit for what sales, demonstrations, and other leads I got from the show. Every time I participated with an owner, she became a very loyal customer.

If you choose to exhibit in the exhibition tent, see the tips on Exhibits and Events.

Hotels

When you leave your room for the housekeeping staff, leave the customary tip AND some literature, samples, and a gift certificate. A sincere thank you note is appreciated when appropriate (for good service). Hotel housekeeping is not the best paid job, so these people are great possibilities for a new member of your team.

Even if no business is generated, you are giving another person a sincere compliment; someone who normally does not get written praise from the public. You also give a great impression of you and your company!

Also see: tips

Home Owners Association

Many planned-unit developments have a home owners association, and with this is usually a **homeowners newsletter**. The newsletter is a great for advertising. The cost is usually very affordable, and because the audience is small, it's more personalized. Ask the association for the advertising rates and also get a **directory of the residents as well as copies of each of the newsletters**. You'll want copies so that you know your ad is printed correctly. And, when new residents are featured, you'll have that information to put together a welcome basket. When you have a directory of all the home owners, you can do some follow through phoning or send your own direct mail pieces to enhance the newsletter advertising.

Many associations have fairs and expos during the year, and they like both residents of the city and of their area to participate. If an association does not offer these, you really should suggest it. The ones I've participated in charge a very nominal fee for a table; thus, if they act on your suggestion, they will have another source of revenue.

Some associations limit their advertising to residents only (very unfortunate for everyone!) If this is the case, you'll want to recruit someone from this area very quickly!! And, even if you find this is the policy, you can still ask. Money talks and many associations like to have the money in their coffers for the upkeep of their facilities.

Speaking of upkeep, if you find that the association is looking for additional funds, offer them a fund raiser. This is a great way to get into the area and meet the residents.

Hospitals

Hopefully you won't find you or your family members in the hospital for any reason but for the birth of a baby. However, most of us at some time will be a patient or guest of a patient in the hospital. Always be prepared with your literature. You never know when the opportunity for doing business will present itself. Let me share a personal example.

I began my direct selling business when I had just one son. Two other boys were added to our family in the following years. During my second pregnancy, I worked extra hard, hoping that the more I worked the faster the time would go. Was I ever wrong!! Well, the day finally arrived. When I went to the nurse's station on the maternity floor, just ready to burst, the nurse on duty turned around and said, "Oh, my goodness, you're the Tupperware lady!" I affirmed that was true, but all I wanted to do right then was deliver a baby.

After delivery, I was wheeled to another set of nurses. By now, I am exhilarated but exhausted, and I know I didn't look like a sales professional--I didn't want to!!! The nurse this time saw me and said, "Aren't you the Tupperware lady?" All I could ask was "How do you recognize me?"

The recognition didn't end there. Once I was settled in my room, I rang for the buzzer for a nurse. Here comes one of the nurses that already knew me, bringing along another nurse, saying, "See, I told you the Tupperware lady was here!" You would have thought I was a famous movie star! And, all I really wanted was peace and quiet!!!

During that stay, several of the other patients on the floor were customers of mine! We had a great time!!

When my husband came to visit me, I told him to bring the product kit and catalogs, I was going to sell something!!

Less than two years later, I gave birth to our third son, Christopher. Guess what I packed in my suitcase this time! Like I said, always be prepared even if you're not planning on doing business.

You just never know when someone will recognize you (even when you don't want them to) and will want your product.

Through the years I've found that people in the medical professions buy a lot!! Nurses are usually a closely-knit team, and when they have demonstrations, a lot of product is sold.

When you do visit hospitals, always leave a catalog along with the magazines in the waiting room. If your product is health-related and disease-preventative, this is a prime place for you to be seen. You never know who will pick it up!!

Honorary Days

Everybody loves to feel special, and we all want to be appreciated. Meet new leads by creating and celebrating honorary days. These celebrations can occur while you're at events, parks, grocery stores, over the phone, any time you have interaction with people who you'd like to meet and help to feel special.

Let me explain how I started honorary days. A few years ago, I was working with my sales team at a county fair. The fair was held in the hot, humid days of August. I noticed several people walking past our booth with whom I would have loved to have talked to and done business with.

One was a mom with a young toddler as well as a baby in the stroller. The other lady was being hounded by her teen-aged children to give them money for the fair rides. Both moms looked tired and worn out. They walked past our wonderful booth. Being a mom myself, I knew that they felt overwhelmed and underappreciated. So, I decided to give them some appreciation.
I walked up to the young mom, gave her a coupon for our product and a token gift and said, "Today is Mom of Toddlers day at our booth, here's a free gift. Please stop by and visit us." All of a sudden, her despaired look changed, she came to our booth. She realized someone cared about her. As I visited with her, I found that she was stressed. She was in the midst of a divorce and couldn't afford our product because of tight finances. So, now I knew what her problem was, and I had a solution. We set up an appointment to share our business plan with her. We were an answer for her!

I used a similar approach with the mom with teens. "Congratulations, today is Mom with Teens day at our booth. Here's a gift for you; please stop in and visit us," I said. She did, and she scheduled a demonstration.

Finding ways to recognize someone is easy. Just look at them; be aware, and then recognize them. Here are some additional ideas:
--lady with red shoes day
--senior citizens day
--pregnant woman day
--dad day
--blue shirt day
--sandal day

Health Club

You can meet a lot of new customers at the health clubs. One way is to **wear your company's logo wear.** Many companies have casual and activewear with their logo. Because you are in a causal atmosphere and tend to see the same people time after time, people will ask questions about your product.

After taking a water aerobics class one morning, I was doing my hair and make up in the dressing room of the health club. I had all my equipment in a duffel bag with my company's logo. A lady standing next to me saw my bag and asked if I was affiliated with the company. Upon my affirmation, she asked if she could have a demonstration with me. Her demonstration was over $1,000 and several people scheduled demonstrations from that one and future demonstrations. I made thousands of dollars and gained hundreds of new customers from carrying that bag.

I still have a jacket I love with a company logo on it. People still stop me and ask me for that product! You'll be amazed at the way logos can become magnetic.

Because you do get to meet new people at the health club, you'll establish new friendships who will become potential customers. You can use some of the other ideas in this book such as displays, drawings, etc. to help you get more leads.

This is great if your product/service is health related. You can use other ideas from this book to promote your product (i.e. the display kit), give out samples, etc.

Holidays

We are a celebrating society! Add to the celebrating by gaining new customers.
Also see: Halloween, Labor Day, Easter, Independence Day

MY OWN LEAD-GENERATING IDEAS:

I

Independence Day

To celebrate the Fourth of July this summer, see how many different states you can get orders from. Ask for referrals from everyone you talk to see if they know people from the states you don't have friends in. It's a great way to celebrate the wonderful country we live in which gives us the freedom to have our own businesses!

Sending a video with catalogs and order forms in even more fun and effective!

Also see: videos

Internet

A web page is nice to refer people to who already know about your business to get more information. Or, if you have links from other sites, you'll have visitors. Many corporations of the direct sellers have their own sites and do not allow individual distributors to have their own. If you can, then do it.

A *TWIST* on having people visit your site is to visit theirs. When you are surfing the net, put in some key words of the kinds of people you would like to do business with. You can do an e-mail right then or follow through with a phone call using selling steps. Remember, you are a GO TO business. Don't depend on people coming to you--GO GET THEM!!!

MY LEAD-GENERATING IDEAS:

J

Jewel Mail

Why do people complain about junk mail? Because they believe that it is junk. Change your TWIST on this and a whole new world opens up. You'll now look at this as **jewel mail.**

Why is it jewel mail? Because the mail becomes valuable to you in the following ways:

1. See how other people are marketing their products. Are they using creative mail pieces that could be adapted to your business?

2. What do the pieces say? Collect those that just "grab" you. Maybe a headline could be adapted to your product. I am not suggesting to steal ideas, but to adapt them. And when you do a TWIST on looking at this jewel mail, you'll come up with new ideas of your own.

3. Local business that you could do cross-promotions and barter with.

4. Is this a medium that you'd like to advertise in? Call other businesses and see if they liked the medium.

5. Keep this organized in a file according to how you'll use the pieces.

6. And, if you like what the advertiser has to offer, patronize them.

MY OWN LEAD-GENERATING IDEAS:

K

Kids

Let your kids help you advertise your business. They can deliver flyers, tell their friends and friends' families about your business.

Do a mom/daughter or mom/son, dad/daughter, dad/son etc. demonstration.

Center a demonstration around kids. If you sell kitchen items, plan a class for teaching children how to cook. If you sell books, offer a parent/child story hour. The idea is that kids attend and want to buy your product, and they bring their parents along.

Key Chains

Be on the lookout for unique, personalized key chains. A good time to buy these is when you find a close out sale. Usually the ones that haven't sold are those with really unique names; these are the new customers that you'll be looking for. Put the key chains on your personal key ring. This will make your keys heavy, and every time you use your keys, you'll be reminded that you need to find these people. When you're standing in line, at a demonstration, or in any other situation when you're carrying your keys (be sure they are visible), people will ask you about them. If they don't see the keys or ask about them, be sure to tell them what you're doing. Then you can explain that you are looking for people with these names so that you can service their needs with your product/service.

When you do find people with these names, introduce them to you and your business. Even if they don't begin a business relationship with you right then, give them the key chain. They won't forget you, and remember that "No" does not mean never. You now have the potential for future business.

If you don't meet people with these names face to face, ask the people you do meet if they know people with these names. In fact, the best thing is when you have to really hunt for these special people. Because, in the meantime, you are meeting many other potential customers.

Purchase unique key chains when you are in cities other than your own. When I was in Orlando on a business trip, I purchased key chains with the Disney characters. I put these key chains on my own key chain. When I'd be standing in line, at a demonstration, or any of the hundreds of potential business situations I found myself in, my key chain would be a real attention-getter!

Once you give out a key chain, replenish it with another one so you are constantly using this system and gaining new customers.

If your company provides a car as a bonus, you'll want to try this suggestion right away--tell the prospect this is the key chain to the future!

MY OWN LEAD-GENERATING IDEAS:

L

Labor Day

This is a great holiday for recruiting. A week or two before Labor Day, anytime you meet people, ask them if they like to **labor for themselves or for someone else.** Give everyone the opportunity to be his/her own boss! Hand out small American flags with your business card. On Labor Day, you can even do cold calls and present this question.

Lines

Whenever you're standing in line, you have another captive audience to meet and get to know. I've found that people are usually bored while they are waiting, and if something does interest them soon, they become agitated and get upset because of the wait! However, when engaged in a conversation, the time really does go quickly!

You'll meet some great prospects. I've found that the key is to be **interested in the other person** because you'll discover what their problems, wants, and needs are. If you have a product or opportunity that will give them a solution, you've both hit pay dirt! If what you're offering doesn't suit them, ask for a referral and feel pleased that you've found a new friend.

Literature

Literature is any written item about you or your business that you give to people so they will remember you. This includes flyers, business cards, company brochures, and so on. Your literature leaves an impression of you. It must be clean, neat, and have your name and phone number. Other information such as address, fax, and e-mail are also helpful. You will attract customers, and they will have a way to contacting you when you have nice literature.

Lucky Names

This is a great way to meet new friends, add to your business, and give some recognition. Think of three or four different names that you like. These names are your Lucky Names. Now, find people with those names. Let them know you've been waiting for find them!

You can enhance this idea by making "wanted" posters and taking to your demonstrations. When you get your guest lists back for a demonstration, see if any of the lucky names are on the list. Call these people right away and tell them that they are "Lucky Names".

Let's say you'd like to know an Ashley, Ruth, and Katherine. Be watching for people with those names. You really will find them! Have you ever bought something that you knew was unique; no one else had this item. This could be, maybe, a green car. As you're driving down the road, you begin to see green cars all over! My opinion is that what you begin to look for, you will find. So, decide on some names and find the people who match the names!

Laundry Mat

Doing laundry probably isn't anyone's favorite hobby, but when laundry can't be done at home, this chore is even worse! When you visit laundry mats looking for leads, you can choose a couple of different idea.

Remember that you have a captive audience because people have to sit and wait for the washers and dryers to do the work while they sit. Give them something to do. Leave catalogs, tear pads, business card bulletins, etc.

If you have the experience of having to do your laundry there, use your time wisely and put these ideas to use. This is a great place for recruiting because you have an opportunity where people can earn money to buy their own washer and dryer. Maybe they live in an apartment and don't have room for laundry. You have an opportunity to help them save to get into a house! Sometimes people do laundry at a laundry mat because their washer is broken.

Once again, you have a great opportunity to help them.

If your product is related to cleaning clothes, homes, etc, this is doubly great for you--and more importantly--for the new business you'll meet!

Library

One way to grow your business is to expand your mind. I recommend monthly trips to your local libraries. How does this bring new leads to you? Check out books that are related to your product/service. Obviously, you will learn from them. And, you know that you don't want to mark your place in the book by turning the pages down, right? So, what should you use for a bookmark? Your business card works really well, or any small piece of literature, brochure.

When you return the book, leave your bookmark in the book for the next person. When the next person checks out the book, not only do they have a bookmark, you have a target audience for your product! If you sell kitchen items, check out cookbooks for new ideas and leave your "bookmark" in the book. When people think of the book subject, they'll relate it to you and want to give you a call!

Newspapers from other communities around the country are often at local libraries and will allow you to find leads.

Reference Section. You'll find the directories that cross reference the residences in your areas with names and phone numbers. You'll also find phone books from around the country so you can expand your business base.

Also see: newspapers

Linger Longer - and Earlier

Get to know people. One way is to attend anything that you're invited to; from a club meeting to a home party demonstration. When you attend these functions, arrive early. Get to know who is in charge of the program or who is the demonstrator. Listen carefully throughout the program Do any of the people in the room have needs that can be met by your product or service? After the function is over (please be careful and don't intrude on the program at hand), get to know those people you have targeted.

Logo Wear

Check with your company to see if they offer logo wear. We are a label-conscious society, and people look at clothing that have logos on it. This is another way to attract attention so people will inquire about your business.

MY OWN LEAD-GENERATING IDEAS:

M

Magazines

Before I began my direct selling career, one of my biggest pleasures was to get a woman's magazine or two in the mail. Then I savored the time I could lie down on the couch while my son was napping, watch soap operas and read about other people's interesting lives! I was bored!

Thank heavens I discovered direct selling and started my own business! Now, I am living an interesting life, and I use magazines, all sorts of them, to find business leads.

Every magazine has a target audience. Your assignment is to match your target audience (Who Cares about your business product?) to a magazine with the same type of audience. Remember above all as you're extracting leads from this source, to ask yourself "What do I have to offer this person that would improve his life and/or solve his problem?"

Some features are universal to all magazines, and some magazines have specialty features and columns. Here are some ideas for getting leads from magazines.

Letters to the Editor. People who write to the editor do so to voice an opinion--an agreement or disagreement. Some times they share personal experiences that lets you get to know them. How can you help this person? Do you just want to write a complimentary or congratulatory letter? How do you get in touch with them? Some writers have a e-mail address which makes corresponding very easy. Most have a city and state listed. You can look them up in a phone directory at the library.

Tips to Share. This is a reader's forum for sharing ideas related to interests of the magazine audience. Use the tip and then write a note thanking the person. Enclose some of your literature.

Many tips I've read are solutions that my product could have solved easier than the solution the reader gave. You can write them to show how your product can help them even more. Send a sample if available and appropriate.

In some of the women's magazines I've read tips about how to keep brown sugar fresh by putting a piece of bread in with the sugar. If you sell a product that keeps food air-tight, eliminating the need for this bread tip, this is a great opportunity to send a catalog along with a coupon that can be redeemed with an order. I've also read many makeup tips that could easily be solved using products sold by direct selling skin care companies.

How to articles. Every magazine is full of "how to articles." Read the article thoroughly, and learn from it. Then ask yourself, "What information could I share with the author that would add to his information?" Do you have a product that would solve one of the problems presented in the article? Your business opportunity might even be of interest to the author.

An author who wrote an article about cutting a family's food budget might be very interested in your coupon redemption business. You could contact the person who wrote "How to Stay Out of Court" if you sell a pre-paid legal service. The possibilities are endless. You can contact the magazine for the address and/or phone number of the author (most work on a freelance basis). My husband is a journalist, and magazines forward responses from readers to him very often. Do keep in mind that not all authors will be open to your ideas, but you'll never know until you try. If they are not interested, do ask them for referrals. Because they are an expert in their field, they might have a gold mine of referrals!

Special Interest Stories. These stories highlight a person or group who has done something of special interest. This person might have begun a community project, volunteered or donated to a worthy cause, or overcome a great obstacle. In this case, you want to contact the person the story is about, not the author. Compliment them on their accomplishment. Show them how you can help their cause. Can you offer a fund raiser to help their organization? Can you donate something to their cause? You don't always have to sell them something. In fact for stories like this, where the featured person has given so much, your contribution would be appreciated, and when you give, you will eventually get.

Recognition Stories. These stories are written to showcase someone's accomplishments. The story could be a multi-page cover story or just a small blurb hidden among other text. You have to be a detective! Since the person is being highlighted because of an accomplishment, a complimentary or congratulatory note would be appropriate. Of course, include your business card and other literature.

"I'm looking for..." Some magazines have an open column for readers to ask the general readership for information. I've seen columns asking for recipes, computer and car parts, best places to eat, on and on... Perhaps your product/service would fill this person's need. Maybe you just have an answer to their question and will send along your literature.

Classified Advertising. This is a great place to find businesses to cross promote. Remember, these advertisers are targeting the same market that you are. How could you join together and help one another?

Contests. Magazines often run contests in conjunction with their advertisers. The winners are then announced in the magazine. Write the winners a congratulatory note. Enclose your sales materials.

Malls

This is not a suggestion to go soliciting up and down the malls. Just like grocery shopping, you can do a non-business activity while finding business leads.

Salesclerks are the first group I become aware of--not for buying, but for selling--my product. When you have received some really good service, acknowledge and thank the person and offer them a gift--your product or service. This could be a catalog, sample, or service that you give to them.

If you really like the salesperson and would like to work with them, tell them so. One idea is to say something like, "you have been so helpful, you seem to really enjoy what you're doing for a living." In most cases, they don't enjoy their job and will tell you. These are prime people to set an appointment with to tell them about your opportunity (don't do it on their employer's time).

If they truly do love their job, ask them if they'd like another stream of income. Here's an approach:

"You have been so helpful today. You seem to love your job."

They reply: "Yes, I really do".

You say, "would you like to hear how you can make an additional stream of income?"

Remember, don't be pushy, but don't be a pushover.

The second group could be people you meet while shopping or waiting in line--especially those who seem to have an interested in or buying items that are complimentary to your product/service. For example, if you sell health-related products and see someone at the sports equipment store purchasing weights, let them know you can help them with vitamins and nutrition. Remember, however, these customers belong to the retail store they are visiting. All prospecting of this type needs to be natural and nonchalant--- during the course of your doing business with this merchant. The best thing is to get your contact's phone number and arrange to explain your product, service, or program at another time. This technique just helps you identity your target market.

Magnets

When meeting new customers, I like to do the door-to-door approach in a neighborhood that I'd like to work in. As I go around and meet people, I leave those who are the most interested a magnet with my name and phone number. If the house looks inviting, but the residents are not at home, I use a magnet to put a flyer or other sales literature on the door. Most newer homes have steel doors and this will hold a magnet. People will call you back because this is such a unique idea.

Money Bag

Instead of carrying a purse or wallet, carry your money and sales literature in a money pouch. You don't have to carry a lot of money, but this is a real attention getter. People, particularly those who wait on you and who wait in line with you will ask you about this unusual way of carrying your money. This is great for getting new recruit leads. You can tell them that you make so much money it won't all fit in your wallet! Then, you'll have your sales material ready to hand them , and all you'll need to do is the follow through! Sometimes, you can even get a recruiting or sales message printed on the vinyl bags. Use a question that will cause others to ask you about your job.

Also See: Purse/Pocket Presentation

Mementos

A memento is something you give to customers and potential customers that is inexpensive to you, yet very valuable to your customer. They won't throw the item away, but will use it often. **The memento must have your name and phone number on it.** Examples are calendars, printed inspirational thoughts, bottle openers, magnets, pads of papers, etc., etc. Give these to people you meet to open up a conversation, as a thank you for their time, order, or referral. Look in the yellow pages under Advertising Specialties for vendors of these products.

Messages

The message you leave on your voice mail and those you leave on the voice mailboxes of others can create new leads for you.

Recorded messages for incoming calls. Leave a commercial on your voice mail so that people calling you will know about your business and current promotions. You're paying for your phone regardless if you do a commercial or not, so you might as well benefit from incoming calls.

I call a lot of people who have direct selling businesses in their homes. Only a small number of these have commercials on their voice mail. Hurry now and create a commercial that will cause great interest in your product and opportunity. Change the message often, and don't keep a message with old news.

Leaving a message on outbound calls. The rule is to always leave a message. Years ago, I would hang up on answering machines because I was afraid the people wouldn't be happy that I called--I had to change my mindset and up my belief in myself and my product! Believe in what you're doing, and others will be thrilled to hear from you.

The next reason I leave a message is because so many people have caller identification; they'll know you called even if you didn't want them to know! Leave a message that will **make them want** to return your call. I have left messages that say
"I have to tell you some news you've been waiting for."
"I have a surprise for you." (people love surprises and want to know what the surprise is--now!)
"You won't believe what I have to tell you!"

I usually say, "I'll be calling you back, or for your reference, my phone number is 553.1212." And, do call them back--if you can beat them to the phone. Most of the time, people will call you because they want to know what the news is!

Leaving messages works well on cold calls because if the people are interested in your offer, they really will call you back. If not, you haven't wasted a lot of time and energy. In this case, my script is a little bit different.
"This is Christie calling from _____(your company). We have a half-price offer this month. To find out more, call me at _____(your number).

MY OWN LEAD-GENERATING IDEAS:

N

Name Tag

Your company's name tag is one of the best advertisements you can have. Think about this. When you're walking around a store and see someone wearing a name tag, doesn't that draw your attention to that person? You really are attracted when you notice that the name tag is not that of the store that you are in. So you look twice as hard. Many times I walked in to a store on my way home from a demonstration and forgot that my name tag was on me. People always question by saying something like, "You work for _____. Do you have a catalog?" What a simple, easy, and I know from experience, very profitable way of attracting new leads.

Neighborhoods

We are a global society, but let's not forget our own neighborhoods. You'll really find gold right in your own backyard! Here are some ideas to make new friends and extra profit:

Let everyone in your neighborhood knows what product/service you sell. I can tell you from personal experience how embarrassing it is when you receive an invitation to a demonstration or business presentation from your neighbor for the exact product or service that you sell! Out of courtesy, I attend the event and get ideas from the other consultant.

One way to spread the word is as soon as you move to a new area or begin your new business, **host an open house/grand opening** showcasing your products. Go personally to each person's home and introduce yourself. If the person is not home, leave an invitation. Do all you can to get the person's phone number so you can personally remind her. I've heard many, many experiences where people have mailed out and distributed hundreds of flyers for these events and only a couple of people show up. Remember that direct selling is a relationship business. People will do business with you when they know who you are and that you care about them.

To encourage business from your neighborhood, put a **yard sign** out that says _____ sold here. You'll want to check for local ordinances concerning signs as well as the use of your company's name if you don't already have rights to use the name/logo.

About every six months, have an annual and semi-annual **Neighbor Appreciation Day** where you only invite the neighbors for specials on your products. Of course, encourage them to bring friends, but the personal invitation only goes right to the neighbors. Make them feel special because they are *your* neighbor!

Neighbors of your customers. I've noticed that some of my customers don't even know their neighbors. If I know this is the case, when I am visiting with my customer, I will make a point to drop by the people on both sides of my customer and tell them about my product.

I have also done this when I've scheduled an appointment with a customer or prospect and they have forgotten and weren't home. I didn't want my trip to that neighborhood to be wasted, so I visited with the neighbors instead.

Networking

My husband, Bob, and I have had the opportunity of playing "matchmakers" with a few couples. Seeing people in happy relationships brings us joy knowing that we were the vehicle to their meeting. Matchmaking is networking.

You have people who you do business with who might need the expertise of someone you know. By networking, you "line" these individuals up. Now, you all benefit! Someday, the people you do business with will know someone who needs you and will be the vehicle for referring someone else to you. An excellent book to read on this subject is *Dig Your Well Before You're Thirsty* by Harvey Mackay (read all of his books for great ideas!) .

75

Newspapers

If you had no other source for leads in a new town, you could build a huge business just by dissecting the newspaper. My husband knows that whenever we travel, I always buy the local papers so I get a feel for the community--and to get leads for my business! If you do want to expand across country without leaving your city, many local libraries have recent copies of other cities' newspapers.

Large metropolitan papers are very helpful; however, the smaller community papers seem to be a little more personal for getting to know people. A combination of both works best!

Births. This section lists the new babies born along with the *parents names*. If families are your target audience, you've found a real gold mine!!

Some of the very best consultants I ever recruited were found from new baby lists. One, in fact, is still a dear friend. I met Tina through this process right after her first baby was born. She didn't agree to doing business immediately, but I faithfully called her back at the times she requested. She scheduled a demonstration and *asked me* about joining my team. Eventually she promoted to a management position. Even though we don't work together any more, we keep in touch. She is now expecting her fourth baby; this idea is very fertile!!

File this section of the paper for a couple of weeks so that you're making these calls four to six weeks after the birth--if you call too soon, the parents will be really tired and might not be open to talking. During this waiting period, look up their phone numbers in the phone book.

When I call, I generally make no reference to the fact that they have a new baby. I just want to know if they want my product. However, I have, at times, approached the call as a congratulatory one and offered to bring a gift by for the new mom. For me, that took more time than I could spend. But, you might want to use that approach. If you have an obvious product for the new baby market, you'll be welcomed with open arms. The new moms might not want to discuss your business right then so be prepared to call them back at a later time like I did for my friend Tina; it's worth the effort.

Community Calendar. Each paper seems to have a different name for this section; however, it is where meetings for clubs and organizations are listed. Which of these groups would care about knowing you and buying your product? You could offer to do a presentation to the group, a fund raiser, volunteer, or even join the organization if appropriate.

Recently, I was introduced to a new group, American Association for Young Families (AAYP), by reading about them in this section. I am presently working on a plan where they can cross promote with a company I consult for, and all parties will benefit.

Business Section. Read more than just the stock listings when you check out the business section of your paper:

New hires and recent promotions in the local business community are often listed; sometimes with a picture and brief business biography. Send a note of congratulations to the person; enclose your business card. At a later mailing or phone call, talk business more specifically. This is a wonderful way to network and to get referrals. Pay special attention to the "who cares about my business" audience. If the person was transferred from another city or state, offer a welcome basket.

Grand Openings of New Businesses. Send the new business owners a "welcome and best wishes for success note." Do you see any possibilities for cross promoting and/or bartering?

Meeting and Seminar Announcements. Expand your business by attending meeting and seminars where you can learn and earn through networking with other professionals. As I read my paper's business section, I am amazed at the assortment of professional meetings. Which group could use your product/service?

Awards and Recognitions. Business owners, especially those working with small companies, love to be awarded and recognized. When you see stories of this nature, send a congratulatory note acknowledging their accomplishment. Enclose a business card. Do follow through contact for business development possibilities.

Achievements. Whenever you read about someone being recognized for personal, business, or school achievements, a congratulatory note is in order. Just like I just told you in the above section, send a business card with your note. In the next contact--via phone, e-mail, mail, fax, etc--offer them your service or product. Pay attention to children and teens; they are now part of a huge demographic buying group.

Fund raisers. When a church, civic, school, or other group is hosting an event to raise money, the local newspaper usually carries an article. If the article lists a contact name, call that person to offer your type of fund raiser. Perhaps you'll want to attend the event to find out more about the organization. Support fund raisers as much as you can to get close to the decision makers for their next fund raiser.

Classified Ads. Just as this section is divided into many subsections, so there are many different avenues to find leads.

Those who are *offering their business services* are prime prospects for recruiting, selling, and possible cross promotions. I always check out the ads for people advertising child care. These people want to work out of their home--great for recruiting! When you read an ad, ask yourself, "What can I offer this person?"

Garage Sales. For more details, turn to this section.

Houses for Sale by owner. This is the section that all real estate agents read first hoping that they will get to convert this property to their listing; this is effective. If you're not a real estate agent, what does someone who is moving need? Do you market lawn care of house cleaning services? Do you sell furniture or home decor? If nothing else, you'll know which homes are for sale. When you know the home has been sold, you have a new homeowner to meet who will want to know what product or service you offer.

Society Page.
Wedding and Engagements. Is your target audience newly engaged or married couples? Do you offer a bridal registry or give bridal showers? Here are names to call! The society page is usually where you can find out the information. One store in my area lists the couples who have registered on their bridal registry. Look these names up in the phone book.

Anniversaries and Birthdays. Send the couple celebrating the anniversary a card. Do the same for the birthdays. Enclose your business card and a coupon for your product. I've seen some papers with baby pictures of one-year olds. Send the baby a birthday card and an offer for the parents.

Reunion listings. These are mostly in the community papers. See which group is having a reunion. Do you have a way to help them during their festivities? Maybe your presentation could be the entertainment. If not, ask what the entertainment will be. If they are doing an auction or drawings, offer them your product as a free or discounted gift, just be sure you get the name and phone of the winner.

Obituaries. This is obviously a sensitive area. Just like the baby list, I would not call anyone right away. I read the obituaries carefully; I want to know if any of my friends or customers, or their relatives are listed here. If so, I send a sympathy card with a copy of the obituary.

For those I don't know, I read for information. I've seen a lot of young widows and widowers. Maybe my product will benefit them in the future. They might be looking for a business opportunity to supplement the lost income of the deceased spouse or to get out and meet people. Direct selling has been real therapy for me to focus on something positive. If you sell life insurance, here's a key place to find prospects. I want to emphasize the need to be sensitive and give the survivors some healing time before you approach them.

Advertisements for companies to cross promote. The newspaper is chock-full of advertisements; large and small ones. Many small businesses use this advertising medium. Read the ads carefully, can you offer the business some cross-promotion opportunities. Would your product or service fill a need for them? These advertisements also give you great ideas for your own direct selling campaigns.

New People in the Area

People who are new to an area feel lost and alone. Having moved across the country more times than I want to count, I know people feel this way! A friendly "hello" and "welcome" from anyone is appreciated!

Look in the Club listings of your local community paper for any formally-organized clubs that cater to the needs of new people. The New Comers Club is one such organization. I have done fund raisers for this organization before, and they go very well because the new people tend to be very cohesive. And, most join for at least a year. You can offer to do a presentation to the group for one of their monthly meetings to begin to establish a relationship with the club. The real key, however, is to meet the new people as they join. This way you can personally welcome them to your area with a welcome basket. Ask the club officer for a listing of the new members.

Some areas have **services that will send out mailings or deliver samples** to new residents. For a fee, you can include your information. If you choose this, be *positive* that you will get the NAPEF of all the people that receive the mailing so you can do your own follow through.

Also see: Welcome Baskets

MY OWN LEAD-GENERATING IDEAS:

O

Organizations

What organizations are you currently a member of? Who in this organization needs your product/service. Just as I mentioned letting everyone in your neighborhood know about your business, let everyone in the organizations to which you are a member know who you are and what you have to offer them.

What organizations out in the world would be compatible with your product? For instance, if you sell vitamins and nutritional supplements, join an organization that is actively involved in this type of effort.

Keep in mind that organizations of all types are looking out for raising funds; can you solve their need?

Also see: clubs, fund raisers, newspapers

MY OWN LEAD-GENERATING IDEAS:

P

Parking Lots

Parking lots are not only full of cars, but also full of golden leads. Leaving business cards or flyers on cars works.

One thing that I love to do in parking lots is meet people. I simply walk up to someone I'd like to meet--usually when they are leaving a store and don't seem to be rushing--and ask them if they have received my free gift. This is an attention-grabbing question. The gift can be magnets with your advertisements, recipes, bookmarks, anything they will want to keep and that they can refer to with your name on it. Remember the gift doesn't have to cost a lot, but it must be valuable.

If they haven't received the gift (I already know they haven't; I just use the question to get their attention), I tell them I represent _____ company, and I'm looking for people who need my product. I ask if they want to be on my mailing list. If so, I quickly write down their NAPEF. By *my* writing this information, they don't have to put down their bags, children, etc. I usually have some sort of coupon, flyer, or catalog to give them on the spot. When I call back, I have them refer to this, and get the order, schedule an appointment for a demonstration and/or business presentation depending on their level of interest.

Parks

If you have children and love the out of doors, you'll love this one! Take your children to the park, and near where your children are playing, set up your product display. Believe me, if your product is something other parents and families can use, people will come by to see what you have. If you did this just once a week every week in the summer, your business would boom. Just remember to keep an eye on your kids or hire a babysitter to come along.

The park is also the perfect place for your hostess to choose to host her demonstration. She loves this idea because she doesn't have to clean her house (one major reason people don't schedule demonstrations), and the guests can bring the kids! This is a great place for a daytime demonstration. You might find that you have to do your presentation in shifts. While some parents are listening to you, others keep an eye out for the children and vice versa. You'll find that once you start doing park demonstrations, others will schedule the same type.

Post Cards

Similar to what I suggested with notes, but even easier! Post cards stand out from the regular mail that people receive (most companies don't send their bills out on post cards!).

Use these colorful, fun pieces of stationery to thank, compliment, appreciate and recognize people. Post cards are easy to keep in a purse or brief case for quick notes. You can hand these out on the spot, or mail them. Your name and company name needs to be on the post card. Postage is less, too.

Anytime you can boost someone's self-image, they will always remember you and your thoughtfulness. Be careful to always be honest; don't send these solely with business motives in mind. This is like the golden rule, treat others like you'd like to be treated and everything will come back to you!

Contact The Booster at 1.800.5JENNYB for great, inexpensive post cards for all the reasons I've mentioned.

Post Office

As a business person you will be making frequent visits to the post office. Be very observant while waiting in line. I look at what kinds of mail people are sending. If they have a lot of packages, I ask if they have their own business. Many times the answer has been yes, and I get to network with this person.

Watch for people who are sending bundles of mail. I've discovered that this person is working for someone else. I comment that he must love his job (I always make that assumption and let them tell me otherwise!). If the answer is no, I ask if he is interested in finding out about my company.

Get to know the postal employees. Let them know what kind of business you have, comment to them about your successes. Invite them to do business with you and to tell others about your business. After all, they talk to people all day. Have them keep you in mind.

Pregnant Women

Watch for pregnant ladies--they're usually easy to spot. This is one of the strongest networking groups I've met, as well as have been a part of! Moms and moms-to-be love to get together and compare notes. You can be the "matchmaker" for moms to meet other moms.

Every other month (or as you want to schedule it), plan a demonstration just for pregnant women. Have invitations that are just for this event. As you meet a pregnant lady, tell her what company you represent and that you do this in celebration of moms. Find out her due date and plan to invite her in about the seventh month--enough time before the baby is born, but when she's tired of being pregnant and wants some special attention! Adapt your demonstration to the needs of the new mom and new child.

Check with obstetricians' offices, maternity shops, and kids' clothing and toy stores, to see if you can advertise this celebration. Remember that new moms make great recruit leads. After the baby comes, they hate to take the child to day care, yet they still need the money they were used to making, and with an extra member of the family, they need even more.

What if you're the pregnant woman? I've gone through two pregnancies while I've been involved in direct sales. I've also known a lot of other pregnant women who ran their own businesses. The funny thing is that while I was pregnant, I attracted a lot of pregnant hostesses, customers, and recruits. My opinion is they thought if I could do this while being pregnant, so could they!

The best benefit of having your own business and being a new mom is that you can gradually go back to work; I never took a full six weeks off. After two weeks, I was ready to get out and meet customers, but I could only work a few hours a week. And, people really pamper you--let them!

Pre-Schools

Not to be confused with day care centers, pre-schools are specifically schools for children before they enter kindergarten. Many times these will be nationally-known chains, or in many cases, schools that people run right out of their homes. My assistant for many years also had a preschool. If your product is for children, parents, or families, contact the owners of the local preschools. I find that bulletin boards in grocery stores and local papers are the best place to find these. Also, ask parents of children who attend preschools.

If your product is child-oriented, the owner will be very interested. She/he may even want to collect orders from the parents and in turn you can give her hostess credit. These owners are also great recruit possibilities for your product/service.

Product

Next to you, your product and product knowledge are your greatest advertisements. I don't agree when I hear, "the product sells itself." If this were true, I would have been out of business long ago. Knowing and demonstrating your product shows your main concern is solving customers' situations; now merely making a sell--a distinction between a salesperson and a service person! Use your product all the time; know each item thoroughly. Use the ideas in this book to tell the world about how your product will solve their problems.

Publicity

Publicity is **free**; unlike advertising that you pay for. Publicity is using editorial materials to promote yourself and your product. The best way is through a well-written news release. Small, community papers are very open to this kind of news; they always seem to be looking for a story.

Purse/Pocket Presentations

One very effective tool to use when you meet people using the ideas in this Lead Alphabet is a Purse/Pocket Presentation. This is a simple, easy-to-use and easy-to-understand mini presentation that you carry around in your purse or pocket.

Here's what you'll need to create your own mini presentation:
 --index cards, whichever size you want to carry around
 --1/2 inch book ring
 --scissors, glue, your company's literature, sale flyers,
catalogs, markers

You can design the presentation how you want. I prefer to put one index card for each of the following subjects:

 --What's New
 --What's Free (hostess, attendance gifts, purchase with
purchase)
 --What's on Sale
 --Hostess Incentives
 --Recruiting Message
 --Picture of kit
 --Picture of your family
 --A page for writing prospects' NAPEF .

The last page, where you write the NAPEF, is so helpful. When I don't have a current Pocket Presentation, I have to scramble to find something to put this information on. Not only is that an unprofessional way of behaving, I've also lost NAPEFs because I couldn't find the little pieces of paper!

Update your presentation to keep it current! Making this presentation does not take long. Consider working with other consultants to put your first one together; you'll come up with even more creative ideas. As you welcome new recruits to your team, give them a Purse/Pocket Presentation of their own.

When you meet prospects in the parking lot, park, lines, and so forth, you can quickly show--not just tell--the reasons why **now is the best time to do business with you.** The items in your Purse/Pocket Presentation will usually be limited-time offers; create a sense of urgency.

You can make up presentations like this to give to your hostesses and potential recruits. They have all the important information to show people who will attend or order.

MY OWN LEAD-GENERATING IDEAS:

Q

Quick Questions

Asking quick questions for quick responses will get prospects' attention. I find right away if they are interested in what I am offering. However, one question I don't like to use is, "Are you interested in............" They don't know if they are or not because you haven't given them much information, and they can easily say "no." The object is to turn the major benefit of your product or service into a question that they respond positively to. Here are just a few ideas.

Would you like to...........? (attend a demonstration, cut your grocery bill in half, preserve your memories, have an extra hour a day)

Have you received the free.....? (analysis, information, gift, catalog, product) You know they haven't because you haven't sent it yet, but they are now in the thinking mode about your product.

Have you heard of............? (the health system, book club, our sales this week/month)

Do you want to know how to.........? (keep healthy by drinking water, cook gourmet meals in minutes, build a business in your spare time)

MY OWN LEAD-GENERATING IDEAS:

R

Real Estate Agents

Due to the many times that our family has relocated, we have met numerous real estate agents. I've discovered two common denominators among these professionals that can be of benefit to direct sellers:

1. They know who is moving in and out of town.

2. They purchase house-warming gifts for their new buyers

In the section on new neighbors, I gave some suggestions on how you can generate leads from new people in the area. One way to get the names of new people is from these agents. Create an alliance with them to trade referrals. Just as they know the new people moving in, you will meet many people who are ready to list a home and can pass the referrals on to them. Establish relationships with agents in a several different areas.

Gifts for new buyers. In talking with agents and receiving gifts myself, $50-$75 is the average price that real estate agents pay for a housewarming gift. You deserve to have a piece of that pie! Before approaching an agent, prepare two or three different ideas or sets of products that you could offer. Giving a value-added price would be an incentive if the agent buys a certain amount. The biggest advantage is the personal service you can give the busy agent. The added benefit is that you'll know another new customer--the new buyer.

If you don't personally know any real estate agents, getting their names is simple. Just pick up the free real estate magazines at the grocery stores. You'll find hundreds of names of agents! Even if they are not interested in creating this alliance or buying gifts, ask them if they would like your product for their personal use.

Recognition Days

Make up your own holidays to recognize groups of people or events. We have bosses day, secretary's day, nurse's day, and on and on. What kind of day can you make up to promote your business and product? Recently, a company that makes paper plates and cups had a national "Don't Do the Dishes Day." They were encouraging people to use their product. If you sell make up, have a Lipstick Day; if you sell phone service, have a Call Your Best Friend Day.

Recognize groups of people by where they live. I did a lot of travelling as a sales manager and consultant. If I were going to work in a distant city, I wanted to have more than a couple of appointments. Many times I would spend an entire day and night in that city to avoid repeat trips. To build my business, I would call a potential customer in the city and say, "Congratulations, Wednesday, June 10, is Castle City Days with XYZ Company. I'll be holding several demonstrations in your town and have chosen you to be a hostess!" This worked so well. Rarely did I have to say anything else. They were honored that I chose them and agreed to be a hostess. Of course, they were thrilled when they saw all the gifts and awards that they earned!

Do a couple of these recognition days every month. Be creative and fun and people will love working with you.

Recycle

Do you have literature that is close-dated; products that will be phased out or catalogs with a price increase? Normally, you wouldn't hand these out to regular customers. But, don't throw them away. Take this literature and deliver in an area that you'd like to do business in, put on car windows, etc. Check with a local community paper to see what the cost would be to have your catalog, flyer, or other piece of literature included with their paper.

One day when I came out of a grocery store, I found a product brochure on my windshield. The brochure was for a company that I had represented for many, many years; so my interest was piqued!

As I looked at this, I realized that the brochure was a year old! Now, I didn't want anything in that brochure, but I was glad to know a representative's name.

You know that many times people look at your catalogs and never order. Why not use these outdated pieces just to get your name out. And, in the wonderful event that they call to order a particular item that is no longer available, simply say that the offer has expired and offer them an alternative. Or, check with other consultants and see if one of them could help you. Remember, the key is getting your name out. Many people are looking for *you* to service them, not necessarily a particular product.

Referrals

The real benefit of having your own business and selling one-on-one is that your customers tell others about you and your service, and your business grows! You've probably noticed by now that I haven't advised you to spend money on massive advertising campaigns. The ideas I've shared here cost very little in terms of dollars. The price you pay is giving outstanding service and follow through. You are your own best advertisement, and your customers are the next best.

Once you have completed the first business transaction with a customer, ask her who she knows who would benefit from what you offer. I've found that by asking as soon as the transaction is made, you'll get more referrals; this is when the customer is at the height of excitement. Have a system for immediately gathering and tracking the referrals. Writing directly on the order form or agreement has worked for me; when I return to my office, I put the name in my referral system. Many times I've had customers ask me to wait to call their friends till after they've had a chance to tell them about me. This suits me fine; all I ask is they call them that day or the next. Then, you can call the referral.

Give a referral gift to the referrer. If your business is based on demonstrations and hostess credit, you simply add the appropriate gift/dollar credit. Other than that, I don't believe in elaborate gifts.

My motto (you've heard this before) is the gift need not be expensive, just valuable. And, have your name and business name and phone attached to it. I believe that the most meaningful token of appreciation which you can attach to the gift, is a sincere note of thanks and constant, exceptional service and follow through.

Refreshments on Me!!

For fifteen years, I grew a business on a product demonstration system. Every once in a while when I saw a great deal on cake mixes, I would buy several. Then I would add a package of powdered drink mix, wrap the two up together, and at the demonstration, I offered the first two to schedule a demonstration refreshments on me! Upon confirming their demonstration, I gave them the mixes. They didn't always use these mixes for the treats, but I didn't care. They invited me to their home to service their families and friends, and my business grew--that's the key to the mix!

Resource Centers

Resource Centers are places you can leave information, even a mini-display or literature and potential customers can leave their NAPEF so you can contact them. This is usually a business that you are doing some cross promoting with. Or, someone that loves your product/service and wants to be able to refer others to you.

Example of resource centers are tanning and beauty salons, grocery stores, copy shops, auto repair shops, juice bars, dry cleaners, health clubs, video stores, laundry mats....the list is endless!

I start with the businesses that I patronize first. I like to do business with people who do business with me. Because I refer my friends, family and customers to the businesses I frequent, I like them to do the same for my business.

Restaurants

Do you sell a product a restaurant needs and uses such as kitchen ware, stationery, spices, etc. Contact the owner and offer your personal service. If the restaurant is not a target audience for your product, get permission to hang a flyer, leave literature, or have a business card fish bowl drawing for customers.

Do you conduct **sales meetings at a restaurant**? This is a great way of getting to know the employees, and they see firsthand the people you work with and hear of your successes. I used to do a sales meeting at one particular restaurant every month. Everyone at the restaurant looked forward to servicing our group--I used to bring them samples of our product, too! A couple of the servers became our customers through this relationship. It was a pleasure for both parties.

On the other hand, I've seen this work for the detriment of the company. After my weekly sales meetings, a group of our sales team would meet at a local restaurant for coffee and dessert. This was done informally, not as a planned meeting for our company. One day I got a call from the manager of the restaurant telling me that the consultants would no longer be welcome at the restaurant because they were very rude to the servers and never left tips! I was really embarrassed for these consultants. They were leaving such a bad impression of themselves and poor reputation for the company.

Be good to the servers. When they know you represent a business, you are that company to them. Tip generously; especially if you've told the server about your business and all the money you make. Leaving a post card note of appreciation along with your tip, gift certificate or coupon for your product, and business card, will give a great impression of you! If you were pleased with the service, tell the server you'd love to have him/her on your team and get his/her phone number! I've recruited many people this way.

If the service was really poor, visit with the server. Maybe he is really bored. Ask him if he needs a challenge and maybe more money. All jobs are important; however, never make someone feel that your job and position are better than theirs. Your respect for them will mean so much.

Retirement Homes

Retirement homes are usually for elderly people who don't want the hassle of owning their own home any longer, but want to be near their friends. As people grow older, many times they are less mobile.

Offer personalized service right at their retirement home. You can set up a product display in an individual's apartment or in their social area. The people love this because they can shop and socialize without leaving their comfortable environment.

Reverse Selling

One of my more favorite ways of meeting new people is through reverse selling. This is when someone tell you about their product/service, and then you tell them about yours. Most sales people think of asking only their vendors to do business with them (more about that later). I do a TWIST. Anytime you are approached by another salesperson, listen and if you buy, or you don't buy, think how your product could help the sales person.
Just because you don't need/want what they have to offer doesn't mean they don't need your product/service.

Think reverse selling when you read advertisements, listen to TV and radio ads, read direct mail pieces, flyers, bulletin boards, and want ads. Keep asking yourself, "How can I help this person?" You'll find people and businesses to service that you would not have found otherwise.

You can use reverse selling when people ask you about purchasing something for their fund raiser. Listen to them and what they have to offer, then tell them about your fund raising program.

Perhaps you have been a recipient of my reverse selling technique. While doing some research for a seminar, I ordered some information about a direct sales company, who in turn sold my name to a mailing list clearinghouse, who in turn, sold my name to people involved in network marketing and direct selling businesses. Every day I find three to five different advertisements in my mail box. I have really enjoyed reading about so many different companies and business opportunities. However, my philosophy about direct selling is that you need to create **relationships** with people, not a massive direct mail campaign-- hence the reason for the lead-generating, relationship-building concepts in this book!

Now when I get one of these non-personal ads, I reverse the selling and send them a thank-you-for-your-offer-note, and an advertisement for this book. Additionally, I follow through with a personal touch--a phone call (if the advertisement had a phone number.) I know if people invested more time in relationships than money in what looks like the easy way, business would flourish.

Rewards and Recognition

When you're looking for new business, give someone some recognition and a reward, and they'll want to listen to you. Let's say that you haven't done business in a particular town, Edenville, but you'd really like to. Go through your customer lists and see who from Edenville has ordered. Or, use the phone book. When you call that person, use the following ideas:
"Hi, _____(their name). This is Christie from _____(company name). I am offering my customers in the Edvenville area an extra _____(what the gift is) today when you set a time to have a demonstration with me. Would you like the _____(gift--reward).

Or, maybe you want to do a demonstration with someone who works at a school. You remember one person that was a teacher at that school. Use the same idea. "I am offering school teachers an extra _____today when they schedule an appointment with me."

MY OWN LEAD-GENERATING IDEAS:

S

"Same Name"

When I meet someone with my same name--either first or last--I feel a real affinity to that person. And, if they spell their name the same way that I do, it's even more unusual (like the way Christie Brinkley spells hers!). The better I get to know them the more I can show them how I can solve their problems. Anytime you have a commonality with someone, they tend to listen to you more and are more open to your ideas.

Also see: commonalities

Samples

If you have small samples of your product that you can give away, do so. If you don't have samples, you can break apart some sets so you can give small samples (remember, not expensive, but valuable!) When I meet someone, I'll say, "Did you get the free sample of my XYZ product?" Everyone wants a sample. Keep the conversation going, and you'll end up with a new customer.

Scavenger Hunt

Do you remember the scavenger hunts of your youth? You would usually team up with another person and be given a list of some unique items that you had to go find. You can play this game as you grow your business.

Think of the kinds of people you'd like to be doing business with, list them on a sheet of paper. As you meet and talk to these people, get their phone number, have them sign your paper, and give them a memento for helping you! Here are some ideas:

96

--a school teacher	--a nurse
--a room mother	--a bank teller
--someone with a blue car	--a mother
--a day-care provider	--police woman
--someone with blonde hair	--a grandmother
--a person who recently moved to your state	--a delivery person
--someone whose name begins with W	--a newlywed

Now, this list is just the beginning. Continue to add to it.

Schools

You could be a teacher or a volunteer at a school and have a never-ending source of new leads.

Teachers. Teachers are real people. They shop just like everybody else. What is unique about your product that would entice a teacher to want it? Is your product related to a subject that the teacher teaches? What about your opportunity. Teachers are the best in a selling position because selling is teaching. And, most teachers work at school only nine of the twelve months.

Volunteers. Sometimes people volunteer because they don't have anything else to do--and that's not a bad position to be in! However, volunteers do not get paid; your opportunity might be something they can do along with the volunteer work and give them a paycheck.

Volunteer yourself. When I've been a room mother, I was able to meet other moms, told them about my business and started new customer bases. When appropriate, I handed small samples of my product out with the holiday treats. You can also volunteer to teach a class on a subject related to your business. If you sell books, offer to do a special story hour. Maybe you could bring your book display in and let the children leaf through them for an hour or so.

Fund Raisers. Schools are always looking for ways to make more money. I've found that going to individual class rooms and departments (music, athletics, and so forth) in the school is sometimes easier to secure a fund raiser event than going through committees and boards.

School Directories. Use your child's school directory to contact parents of students to tell about your business and product. You can mail information or make calls (I believe in personal contact.)

Service

This book contains literally hundreds of ideas of finding new leads so your business and your checkbook can grow. This is the simplest, but the most important concept of the entire book. Giving good service--in fact, not good, but outstanding and superb service to your customers is **the most important way of growing your business**. When this happens, and you have just one customer, she/he will go brag about you, and you'll forever be in business! Customer service is talked about more today than ever, but not always practiced! Show even your few customers that you keep your promises, deliver more than you promise, and do your very best to solve their problems by using your products. Believe me, people will remember you.

Service People

Another way that I've met new customers is when I've done business with service people. Whenever you have any kind of a service person come to your home or office to do work, tell them about what you do. This could be appliance repair people, plumbers, electricians, and on and on and on.

We hired a builder to construct a home a few years ago, and I was keeping a close tab on all the subcontractors. So, every day I was on site checking on what was going on and getting to know who was building my house. Our painter was real nice. In our conversations, I told him about my business. I asked if he was married (don't ever assume) and if his wife used my product. He said that she did and gave me her name and phone number. His daughter was newly-married and scheduled a demonstration with me. She quickly saw the financial benefits and joined my team. She happened to begin her business during the biggest week of the year. She was the top consultant and made a very large profit. All because I got to know the painter of my house.

In the same house, I had a third telephone line installed; a dedicated line just for my consultants' use (more about that in the Lemon Aid Laws for Leaders book). The phone installation guy came out and spent hours trying to figure out the wiring in my home. As I was helping him, we were discussing the reason for another line in my home. Again, I asked if he was married, if his wife worked, would she like a job like mine, etc. I contacted her, and she too joined my team.

I have many other examples of business derived from sharing my business with people I do business with. If you keep doing this, and add up all the profits and residual profits, you could pay for your repairs and your home by having service people do their job so you can do yours.

Sorry we Didn't Meet

Carry a note pad or have some cards printed up that say "Sorry we didn't have the chance to meet." When you're out and about going door-to-door, or just stopping by to meet someone who is not at home, leave a personalized note. Leave your name and phone so they can call you back. The usually don't, so be sure you follow through and call them.

I also carry some magnets with my name or a catchy phrase on it (call 1.800.5JENNYB for great magnets!) If the house has a steel door, the magnet will stick to the door and hold the note. Another way to get someone's attention.

Sports Teams

Are you a soccer mom or dad? What about baseball, basketball, bowling and so forth? As you watch your children participate in sports, you normally meet and talk with other parents. Let them know about your business. Use your product where they see it whenever possible or practical.

Maybe you're the athlete, or your spouse is, or the both of you? You'll get close to the other team members. Most teams have a few social events during the season. Tell these folks about what you do; always ask for referrals as well. These groups will open up hundreds of lead avenues for you! Of course, be willing to tell your associates about the businesses of your team members so you are really networking.

Surveys

By taking a survey, you will be able to find out what your customers' needs and problems are, and then you can show them how you can help them, you're not just selling them something!

Before you do a survey, **think about the purpose.** Ask questions that will have relevance; not just something that will fill up time and space. Adapt the questions to the audience. Be as specific as you can be for a particular group.

Written surveys. If you are having people fill out something themselves, do a multiple choice survey so they don't have to write a lot. You can also use the rating method where you have them list their interest, satisfaction or other level of thinking between one and a number, like ten--one being the lowest, ten being the highest.

I like to do phone surveys; they have to be quick, and at the beginning they are very general. When I'm writing down responses, I can add more open-ended questions so the person can tell me more about them.

My goal in doing prospect-finding surveys is to find out if the person might be someone "Who Cares" about what I have to offer. If I am selling satellite systems, I would ask, Do you watch TV? Do you own a Satellite System? What brand? Are you happy with the programming? Have you heard about the 24-hour Success Channel? The last question is where I'll begin telling more about my product.

If someone says they are not interested in talking to you, please be polite and thank them.

MY OWN LEAD-GENERATING IDEAS:

T

Telephone

Think of your telephone as your cash register. Every time you dial a prospect's number, or someone calls you, listen to the cha-ching, cha-ching of the money going through.

Outbound calls. The calls you make to prospects and customers will be what builds your business. Make a daily goal to talk to a certain number of people; busy signals and answering machines don't count; you must actually talk to the person and ask him/her to do business with you.

Inbound calls. The more calls you have coming in, the more money you'll make. I suggest getting connected to a voice mail system so you don't miss any of those important calls. I don't suggest call-interrupting (also known as call waiting). I have my voice mail set up so that if I'm on the phone and another call comes in, the new call goes directly to voice mail. This way, the customer I'm talking with doesn't get interrupted, and I don't miss any calls.

Telephone Books

If you ever feel like you are totally out of leads, and you've tried every idea in this book so far (we're almost to the end of this book!), grab the **Ultimate Lead Book**--the Telephone Book. Look at the thousands and thousands of people and businesses listed in the book. Ask yourself, **"Have I talked to everyone of these people?"** I haven't met anyone who has talked to every single person and business in the Ultimate Lead Book.

Calling people randomly from the phone book is known as cold calling. Don't let that term turn you cold! **Some of my best customers have come from this activity.** Let me share a success story with you.

In 1989 our family made a cross-country move from Detroit, Michigan to Salt Lake City, Utah. This is when I first began using a telephone book to find leads. I called a lady by the name of Joy. I told her hello, I'm with _____ and would like to schedule a demonstration with you. Imagine my surprise when she said "sure." I must tell you that this was not the first cold call I had made. More than likely, I had made a hundred or so before I got this yes.

Now I was a little bit nervous because I didn't know her, and I didn't even know where she lived. So, I made an appointment to go meet her and plan her demonstration. I recommend this to everyone. Most of your customers will be nice people in good areas, but I want to know who they are, and I'm sure they want to know who I am *before* I come to do the demonstration. Only one time in my direct selling career did I drive up to a home for a get-to-know-you appointment and then drove off because I didn't feel comfortable. I finally met that person and everything turned out fine; but do be careful.

So, I went to plan a demonstration with Joy. She was like me, a Mother of Boys!! We had a lot in common, and I suggested she join my team (always make that suggestion when you plan a demonstration!). She told me that her youngest son had health problems, and she spent a lot of time driving to the hospital; she couldn't see how she could fit anything else in. I finished with the appointment, and two weeks later went to her demonstration.

As I was walking into the foyer of Joy's home, I overheard her telling the guests that she was now going to sell my product! I almost fell over! This was news--good at that--to me!!

Joy had a great party; we even recruited another person that night. As the story ended, she really was overwhelmed with caring for her son's needs, and wasn't able to continue working on my team. But, the story continues. Here's the Link: From Joy, I had two new people join my team. Both of them were promoted to management in the company. For years after, until I moved from Salt Lake, I had residual business, making thousands of dollars, from that one cold phone call.

When you make these calls, remember that the person on the other end of the phone doesn't know you, and you don't know her. The worse thing that can happen is you'll get "no" for an answer--that is the worst thing!!

A couple of hints that have helped me. When I make the calls, I **ask for the person by his/her first name.** Whenever I get a call asking for "Mrs. Northrup," I know this is someone who doesn't know me but is trying to sell me something! So, if you want to call women, look for their names listed in the phone book.

When I make the call, and the person answers, I energetically say, "Hi, is this Terri?" Well, Terri thinks I'm her friend because I am friendly! I begin building a strong rapport. "This is Christie with _____(your company)." Would you like to know about our specials this month?" If she says "no" ask if she'd like you to call back another time. If she is still not interested, a friendly (not a disappointed-sounding) thank you and good bye is most appropriate.

Notice what I didn't do. **I did not ask "How are you today?"** I'm afraid if I ask them they might tell me! Plus, that is a very tired and trite greeting. Be friendly and get to the point. This way, if the person truly isn't interested, you're not wasting her time or yours!
Notice **I got right to the point**. I figure that if she wants my product, she'll want to know what's on sale. Sometimes, if I feel like there is a real interest mixed with reluctance, I might offer to take some information to her so she gets to know who I am. But be careful with this. Sometimes people tell you they'd like your catalog just so they can get you off the phone.

When the prospect wants to know more, give her the information and then ask for an order, appointment, or demonstration. Most people want to be asked; they usually don't volunteer to purchase.

If your company doesn't offer monthly specials, change the question to capitalize on the strongest benefit that you offer--free cooking classes, facials, cleaner air, better-tasting water...

Cold calling is great. You can make a lot of calls in just a few minutes because you're not being chatty; you get right to the point and find the people who want you and your product.

Telemarketers

Think about this for a minute. In the course of a week, how many phone solicitors call your house? Usually these people are employed by someone else, like your credit card company, phone company, etc. They are normally paid by the hour, and usually don't have a passion for the product they are telling you about.

My number one rule is to always be nice to these people, even if you are not interested in what they are offering you because what goes around really does come around! In other words, if you are polite to these people, people will be polite to you when you are doing your calls.

Last week, one of the many calls I received was from a lady who had just started working for the telemarketing firm. She was *so* nervous! She stumbled over the script (I hate scripts!), and couldn't even remember her own name! I really felt sorry for her. I complimented her on her attempts, and helped to put her at ease. What she was offering me was not something I was interested in (I didn't say you had to buy from these people; just be nice). So, I asked her if she liked her job and if she was getting paid $15 to $20 per hour. When they reply was no, I asked if she'd like to be doing telemarketing where she got the profits and future business instead of someone else. All of a sudden, she did a big TWIST and became very interested.

Thank You Notes

When someone has been very helpful to you as a customer, send them a thank you note and tell them you'd love to have them as *your* customer or even better have them work with you on your team! Most people are flattered by this compliment, and even if they don't become a customer/recruit, will give you referrals. You have to call them back after they've received the note; they don't often take the initiative.

Three Foot Rule

At this point, you've realized that you can build your business by talking to people everywhere. To help yourself remember this, think of the Three Foot Rule. Most people stand about three feet apart when communicating with each other. Every time you get within three feet of another person, find out about them, and tell them how you can help them through their using your product/service.

Tickets

A ticket represents value. Instead of just sending out flyers or verbally inviting people to a demonstration or business presentation, use tickets. Print a price on the ticket. Get a rubber stamp made up that says "complimentary." After printing the ticket, stamp it with this rubber stamp. The person who receives the ticket will feel much more special when you've given them a ticket. And, because the ticket represents value, the ticket-holder usually shows up to the event. They don't want to forfeit any opportunity.

I saw this concept in action. Our community was having a home and garden show. Tickets were advertised as five dollars, or you were advised to get free tickets from a local real estate agent. I kept thinking of which agent I could call to get a ticket. I never called anyone, and decided I'd just pay the money. When I arrived at the event, admission was free. I realized that the agents just wanted people to call them!!

MY OWN LEAD-GENERATING IDEAS:

U

Universities

You'll be amazed at the kinds of contacts you'll find on a college campus. Having recently returned to college to work for a second degree, I've found this to be a potential gold mine. Here are some suggestions and reasons:

1. Advertising is cheap if you want to pay for a classified or display ad in the student paper.

2. Upon approval of the school, you can hang up flyers.

3. College students are usually eager recruits. They are young (or young at heart), enthusiastic, and need money along with a very flexible schedule.

4. College students are very innovative. The ideas for the bathroom stalls were from my recent college experience. That's just one of many I've seen.

5. Local students will refer you to people in the area, many times their parents, for referrals.

6. You can use the club idea aforementioned and address campus clubs.

7. Many colleges have career/job fairs. You can put a display here for a very minimal charge, if any.

8. Register for classes that could be related--even distantly--to your business. Here you'll meet other professionals, learn from them, and invite them to do business with you. Don't rule out the teachers. They are people too, so let them know what your business is.

Also see: events, advertising, clubs

V

Vendors

Which businesses or individuals do you do business with for business or personal needs? My slogan is "I do business with people who do business with me." Are the following people part of your customer base: insurance salesperson, mechanic, child care provider, attorney, dry cleaner, hair stylist... The list is endless.

Go through your checkbook--both business and personal, to see who you've written checks to. Have these people/businesses written one to you for your services? If they aren't part of your customer base, have you told them about your business?

During a short period of time, I was taking my sons to the doctor's office very regularly. When I got to the billing desk to pay, I gave the office workers a catalog and asked which of my products they needed or wanted. The woman who was helping me looked stunned. I said, "I've been writing checks to you regularly, now you can write one to me." They all laughed, agreed, and placed an order.

Remember that some of your vendors might already have someone servicing them with your product or service. Don't harass them; just keep in touch to be sure they are happy with their present vendor, and if not let them know what you can do for them.

Vets

See: waiting rooms

Videos

To expand your customer base to areas outside your geographic area, produce a video presentation. You can personalize this video for a specific group, or do a generic video and mail to many people. I started this during a big challenge week that my company was offering. Because of my cross-country moves, I had customers, friends, and family around the nation. For the big week, I did a demonstration on the video and mailed it to people who wanted to host a demonstration.

The hostesses loved this idea because people could come and go during a block of time, rewind the video, and see the whole demonstration. One group did some "reverse recording." They did a video of the people who attended complete with personalized messages to me and mailed the video back with their orders.

Video Stores

Video stores are good resource centers, especially the ones that are locally-owned and operated. Ask the owner if you can put up a display of your literature or a business card drawing. Most stores have community-oriented videos (safety, health, etc.) available at no cost. Ask to put a video of your products, services, or business plan in the free-to-rent section. Track the names of those who check out the video so you can follow through.

Volunteers

Meet new customers by volunteering your time to organizations that are of interest to you and could be related to your business. Do this to help benefit others, and you'll surely meet new business prospects.

MY OWN LEAD-GENERATING IDEAS:

W

Welcome Baskets

Welcome new members of your community by taking a basket of your product samples and literature. Including pertinent information about your community adds a welcome touch. Check with your local Chamber of Commerce to see what materials they will give you to help welcome these people.

Who cares?

This is called finding your target audience. Take a good look at your product/service. If you could only market to one group of people, who would that be? Ask yourself "Who would care the most about what I have to offer?" Or, "If I could only show my product to one group of people, who would that be?" Once you determine this, get to know people in that group, hang out where they hang out, use the ideas in this book to find more of them.

Wrong Numbers

Have you misdialed a phone number? I have plenty of times. Instead of just apologizing, offer the person your product or service. Try something like this: "I'm sorry for misdialing; I am a consultant with _____(your company). Can I be of service to you?" This might sound far-fetched, but I have results from this!

Old number. People move around a lot. I know from experience! If you dial a correct number, but the customer isn't at that number, use a similar approach: "_____(person you're trying to reach) must have moved. I am a consultant with _____. Can I be of service to you?"

Wrong Houses

Have you ever taken your product kit and gone to the wrong house? If you haven't you ought to try it! Well, I must admit I was embarrassed. The hostess told me her house was yellow. I didn't think that one street would have two yellow houses on it, and I went to the wrong one! Well, what would you have done? I gave the person a catalog and invited her to come to the demonstration! This really is a TWIST on a sour situation that can be turned into sweet successes!

Word of Mouth

Direct selling is all about word-of-mouth advertising. Instead of companies spending millions and millions of advertising dollars, they award consultants to advertise the product. In other words, be good to your customers, they'll tell the world for you.

"Would you like to Attend?"

If your business is based on a demonstration plan, scheduling new demonstrations is critical to building your business. You probably know by now that not everyone wants to be a host or hostess. So, don't get discouraged. **Meet the customers "where they are" before you take them to where you want them to be.** Ask them if they'd like to be a guest at a demonstration. At least this way, they get to know and trust you. And, maybe someday they will be a host or hostess. Remember persistence is what counts, not pushiness!

And, after you have enough people to attend a demonstration, soon you'll have a party! One of those "attendees" might just like to become the honorary hostess and collect all the gifts!

Wish Lists

We all have needs, wants, and wishes. I believe that if you write your wishes down, they will come true; not like making a wish when you blow out the birthday candles on your cake and the wish only comes true when you don't tell anyone!

A wish written is a goal set. So, when your customers look at your catalog and see all the products, they normally want more than they can afford. Provide each customer with a wish list. Have them **make a list of everything they would want if money weren't an object**. Now you know what they want. Have them give the list to you. You take the list and make a copy. Send the guest a copy of the wish list with a note.

My approach was to tell her what my consultant cost for all the items would be. In other words, "everything on your list comes to $100. If you were a consultant on my team, your cost would only be $50. Which would you rather pay?" This approach has helped me recruit a lot of people. Then I had the privilege of going a step further and helping them come up with a career wish list.

Waiting Areas

If you are in a waiting room, that means that you are doing business with some kind of a professional, be this a hair dresser, attorney, dentist, chiropractor or many other professional services. You have to wait for your appointment just as other customers do. Get to know the other customers. Drum up a conversation where you will ask leading questions, but they will tell you all about themselves. Listen carefully to see if you can solve their problems with your product/service.

If your product is something that people waiting can use (magazines, books, toys, etc.), donate these to the waiting room in exchange for the owner letting you put up some flyers. Leave a trail of catalogs on the tables.

You're patronizing them, give them the opportunity to do business with you!   When you get into the professional's office, show them how your product will help them. Offer to give product in trade for their service (bartering). When you check out and pay for the service, talk to the employees about your business.

MY OWN LEAD-GENERATING IDEAS:

X

Xceptional Xamples

You must be a product of your product if you expect others to buy what you sell. Be the best example of your product or service that anyone has ever seen. If you sell Jaguars, be sure you own one yourself! Nothing speaks like the voice of experience. People will believe you more and do more business with you when you walk your talk!

MY OWN LEAD-GENERATING IDEAS:

Y

Yard Signs

Put a sign on your front yard with your company name and logo so people know where they can get your product. Your phone number needs to be on the sign as well.

The side benefit is that when the neighbors are telling their friends how to get to their house, they'll use your sign as a reference. "Turn right at the house with the XYZ sign." You'll be happily amazed at the new people you'll meet.

Year Books

Contact your local schools and dance clubs. Many of these organizations have end-of-year year books---and you can advertise in them! The best way is if one of your children happens to attend one of the schools. You can put a good wish message and advertise your business at the same time. If you don't have children attending these groups, ask about advertising anyway, and stipulate that you want a list of people who are members of the group so you can follow up.

MY OWN LEAD-GENERATING IDEAS:

Z

Zillions of other Ideas

The alphabet is coming to an end, but this is just the beginning of new lead ideas that you'll come up with as you try out the suggestions in this book. I believe that the world is full of links. By starting with these leads--which are the seeds--you'll be linked to an infinite amount of ideas and leads. You'll never be out of business--even if you are out of family and friends.

MY OWN LEAD GENERATING IDEAS:

Are you Thirsting for more Hostesses, Customers, and Recruits?

Invite The Lemon Aid Lady to quench that thirst with classes tailored to you...

Lemon Aid Learning Adventures™ now offers a variety of classes...in different formats...to help you book more demonstrations, sell to more customers, and greatly expand your team with new recruits and more leaders.

On-site Classes
We've adapted our popular Lemon Aid Learning Adventures for team meetings. For groups of 50 or more, we'll come to your location with a two-hour presentation custom-tailored to your company, area, and team needs. Call for details.

Team Telephone Talk
If your group is small, take heart! We offer a 45-minute team talk by phone.

Lemon Aid One-on-One
Personal coaching, Lemon Aid style! In personal, half-hour phone sessions, Christie will help you *twist* your personal Sour Situations into Sweet Successes and Juicy Profits.

Three Options. A myriad of topics..
We offer a wide variety of presentations, including:

Sales	Leadership
• Where to Find Customers when you Run out of Family and Friends	• From Parenting Your Team to Mentoring Your Team
• Presentations for Profit$	• Lemon Aid for Leaders
• Family Fortunes without Family Feuds	• Totally Terrific Teams
• There's No Place Like Working From Home	• Opportunity Meetings with a *TWIST*
	• When Life Give You Lemons, Start a Lemon Aid Stand

Lemon Aid Learning Adventures. Creating Sweet Successes and Juicy Profits!

Lemon Aid Learning Adventures
P.O. Box 1720
Lake Dallas TX 75065
940-498-0995 www.lemonaidlady.com

What Sales Professionals like you are saying about The Lemon Aid Lady...

"My advisors all found you to be an inspiration!...You are a gifted speaker, able to pull in your audience and use them to illustrate your points. They really listened and learned because you made it seem so attainable."

Sherry Clifton, Regional Advisor, Longaberger

"Her Learning Adventure was unique to our Company...Christie's biggest difference is that she talks our language!! She knows sales and what it is to be a sales person...Since the presentation, we've had the following results: Higher Sales and Sponsoring. That alone pays for having The Lemon Aid Lady Learning Adventure."

Eunice Carroll, Diamond Infinity Designer, Home & Garden Party

"Christie's ideas have helped my new unit to think out of the box to find new leads, and this is what's motivated them to go out and find new customers...her Totally Terrific Team concepts now have my team members all excited about bringing recruit prospects to our team meetings!"

Christi Weems, Director, Mary Kay

"At our January Kick-Off, Christie did a wonderful job of teaching ways to help us connect with our crowd, packaging ourselves, and finding commonalties with those in the audience. Her ideas were unique and applicable to kitchen consultants and all levels...91% rated her training session as 'Excellent'."

Robin Rogers, Senior Director, The Pampered Chef

"This seminar was excellent. Every idea was so useful to help build my business. I would recommend this to anyone in home businesses."

Marci Ruff, Tastefully Simple

"Your sharing of personal testimonies really touched my heart because you were sharing from your heart. Thank you for helping me realize why I got involved in direct selling in the first place. May God bless you for being a 'light' to us."

Ute Looney, Weekenders

"My bookings have gone up drastically, having nine from the last two shows. I can't thank you enough...By twisting the way I do my shows, I have realized so much sweet success already."

Linda Home, Pampered Chef

"This is the most concise training I've ever seen that gets to the meat and potatoes of direct sales. It is so simple and easy to follow, a consultant can use it the very next day."

John Chwalek, Tupperware Distributor

Add more Sweet Successes and Juicy Profits with these other Lemon Aid™ Books and Tapes!

Presentations for Profit$

The demonstration is the backbone of a home-party business. But it's more than just presenting products. In *Presentations for Profits$,* you'll learn dozens of ways to increase your bookings and recruit more hostesses at home party demonstrations through creative preparation, presentation, recognition, and follow-through.
$21.95

The Lemon Aid Lead Alphabet: Where to Find Customers when you run out of Family and Friends

Quench your thirst for new business with the ABCs of generating sales leads. This 115-page book is written in an easy-to-use, reference-style format. No need to read the book from cover to cover. Simply turn to any page for easy, creative, no-cost ideas for finding people who want and need your product or service.
$21.95

The Lemon Aid Deed Alphabet

Once you have located leads, what deeds do you need to do to convert them to committed customers? Written in the same format as the *Lead Alphabet*, this 120-page book will teach you what to do to keep your customers committed to YOU and how to it.
$19.95

Totally Terrific Team Themes

Are your team meetings a treat to plan? Do team members look forward to attending the meetings? Does performance increase after a meeting is held? The answers to all these questions will be a firm "yes" when you plan your meetings using the themes in this book.
$19.95

The Lemon Aid Lead Alphabet Tape Series

Do you own the *Lemon Aid Lead Alphabet: Where to Find Customers when you run out of Family and Friends?* Have you attended a live Lemon Aid Learning Adventure with the Lemon Aid Lady? Now you can combine the best of both experiences and hear NEW ideas never before taught in a live session or published in the book. This nearly four-hour audio tape set will teach you the A-to-Zs of finding customers in unlikely places with innovative *TWISTS.*
$55.95

Prices and product availability subject to change without notice.

Lemon Aid Learning Adventures. Creating Sweet Successes and Juicy Profits!

Lemon Aid Learning Adventures
P.O. Box 1720
Lake Dallas TX 75065
940-498-0995 www.lemonaidlady.com

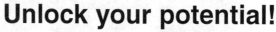